T0063108

[ENDORSEMENTS]

[This is] an excellent testimony of a mother's unconditional love! As Amelia shares her journey through life with her special son, her narration exudes *spirituality* which immersed her in resilience, patience, endurance, physical and emotional strength, self-belief, self-sacrifice, and of course faith and hope – qualities so essential to her daily coping with the uncertainties in the pattern of behaviour of her autistic son.

Amelia is a *super mum*, so deserving of the victory that she; her son, Aaron; her husband; her daughter, Alysha; and her extended family celebrate today!

Dato' Leela Mohd Ali
Trustee and CEO of Penyayang (a Malaysian NGO)

With rare insights, *A Rude Awakening* documents one such case study between a loving mother and her son. Though she is unavowedly Christian in her approach, her journey and struggle to educate her son in basic cognitive skills – with its big triumphs and unremitting failures – cannot help but encourage us to carry on as faithful, pragmatic, and hopeful parents to see the end result even in the small beginnings.

I was very touched by the frank honesty displayed in her testimony. Having experience with autistic children myself, being involved in the Ignatius Catholic Church's outreach to special needs children, I can truly understand her plight in raising an autistic son. In an age when fast results are equated with success, she 'walked' her son at his own pace, not hers. That perhaps holds the key to her breakthrough. Sparing nothing to encourage his growth in whatever interested him remains an unforgettable lesson in giving.

Gladly do I recommend this loving book to all parents of autistic children and those who are called to be encouragers alongside. As the prophet Micah said: 'How can two walk together except that they be agreed?' (Amos 3:3). It is to the mother's credit that she consensually obtained the agreement of her son in their journey of life together.

Reverend Chris Choo
Kuala Lumpur, [University of London (LLB); LSE, London University (Bachelor of Law); Barrister of Law, Inner Temple, London]
Itinerant Pastor, St Peter's Anglican Church, Ipoh
Founding President of MODA (Malaysian Designers Association)
Member of Pastoral Board of WOL (Wealth of Life)

Autism is a lifelong developmental disorder which affects one's ability to relate to his or her environment [as well as] interact with other people. It is characterised by poor social and communication skills and repetitive and restrictive behaviours and interests. Autism has far-reaching effects for a child which flow on to impact parents, siblings, family, friends, teachers, and the wider community.

I see many children on the autistic spectrum in my clinical practice, and every child is different. I cannot imagine the life that goes on behind closed doors, the struggles and difficulties families face day to day. *A Rude Awakening* is an inspirational account of one such family, whose perseverance and unwavering strengths in their Christian beliefs have upheld them through their child's life. Amelia Chin displays the unlimited nature of a mother's love for her son, the one true advocate for a child whose words cannot be heard in this very confusing world of social norms.

Dr Anthony Liu
Consultant Paediatrician (Sydney)

A RUDE AWAKENING

FOR A BOY WITH AUTISM

"I thought I was the one 'normal'
in this world of quirky, 'abnormal' people"

AMELIA CHIN
AS TOLD TO JOYCE HEE

PARTRIDGE
A Penguin Random House Company

Copyright © 2014 by Amelia Chin.

ISBN: Softcover   978-1-4828-2638-8
           eBook   978-1-4828-2639-5

All rights reserved. No part of this book may be used or reproduced by any means, graphic, electronic, or mechanical, including photocopying, recording, taping or by any information storage retrieval system without the written permission of the publisher except in the case of brief quotations embodied in critical articles and reviews.

Because of the dynamic nature of the Internet, any web addresses or links contained in this book may have changed since publication and may no longer be valid. The views expressed in this work are solely those of the author and do not necessarily reflect the views of the publisher, and the publisher hereby disclaims any responsibility for them.

Unless otherwise indicated, all Scripture is taken from the Holy Bible: New International Version Copyright @ 1973, 1978, 1984 by International Bible Society.

To order additional copies of this book, contact
Toll Free 800 101 2657 (Singapore)
Toll Free 1 800 81 7340 (Malaysia)
orders.singapore@partridgepublishing.com

www.partridgepublishing.com/singapore

CONTENTS

Part 3 – At Present

DEDICATION

To my husband, Eu Han Chin, who has stood by me in his unfailing love and understanding; to my son, Aaron, who is God's special masterpiece to me; to my precious daughter, Alysha, who, in her giving and loving ways, has been a vital link to my son's progress and functionality.

To both Aaron and Alysha, I would like to quote Henri Nouwen: 'You are not an accident; you are a divine choice.' Additionally to Aaron, I dedicate this verse: 'In the shadow of His hand He hid me; He made me into a polished arrow and concealed me in His quiver' (Is. 49:2).

And lastly, to my parents and parents-in-law, who have been my constant source of support and love.

Aaron's drawing at age eight

ACKNOWLEDGEMENTS

My special thanks to my mum, Joyce Hee, for writing my story, and to my dad, T.F. Hee, for typing and editing the drafts. My mum is a retired English teacher who has always had a passion for writing short stories and articles.

I could not have written the book myself for two reasons: firstly, time has always been my constraint. Secondly, even if I had the time to write, I would have found it difficult to recall in detail most of the events that constituted the painful part of my life. My mind had instinctively shut off or suppressed the unpleasant hurting memories in the subconscious, possibly as my defence mechanism of denial. My mum was an eyewitness to much of all that was happening, as my parents were with me for months during the most critical periods. She has a vivid recall of the incidents, however minor, possibly because God was preparing her to write this book on my behalf as her vision to glorify God.

To my family members, especially my brothers, sisters-in-law, and god sister, I thank them for providing invaluable feedback.

My mum wishes to thank Sow Yong for inspiring her to write and, most of all, Suyan for her contribution in helping to edit the first draft as well as for her insightful advice.

My greatest tribute is to God, without whom this book would never have been written.

FOREWORD

I was overwhelmed with emotion when I read the chronicles of Amelia's personal life journey, coping with the immense task of nurturing an autistic child. The courage and perseverance she has shown demonstrates not only the loving heart of a mother but also the sacrifices she made for a love that is priceless and rewarding.

Responding to this heart-rending description of Aaron's growth and the struggles of the writer, I am reminded of [this] biblical truth: 'Godly sorrow brings repentance that leads to salvation and leaves no regret, but worldly sorrow brings death. See what this godly sorrow has produced in you: what earnestness, what eagerness to clear yourselves, what indignation, what alarm, what longing, what concern, what readiness to see justice done. At every point you have proved yourselves to be innocent in this matter' (2 Cor. 7:10–11).

A Rude Awakening for a Boy with Autism gives hope to the hopeless, strength to the weak, courage to the despairing, and assurance to the guilty, especially for those who share similar challenges and can identify with the writer's experiences.

Naturally, it is inevitable for us to grieve and to feel sorrowful. The worldly grief caused by the loss or denial of something we want so much for ourselves is self-centred. It laments about not receiving what we think we deserve from God. Such self-centredness, which gives rise to despair, bitterness, and paralysis of our souls, drowns us in self-pity and ultimately leads to a cancerous sore.

The experience of the author demonstrates godly grief. Though she encountered grief and sorrow, she allowed her feelings and struggles to move her into positive actions. She was motivated to go to God and to act compassionately and positively towards Aaron. Her unceasing hope encouraged her to turn the problems around by taking the past tense and allowing God to change it into His future tense.

The book is written candidly, with apt and brilliant advice as well as suggestions for those coping with an autistic child. The competently written narrative introduces a clear understanding of the behavioural patterns of an autistic child and gives pragmatic guidelines to develop the child's potential. The author conveys in amazing and astonishing ways how she successfully overcomes the odds and eventually experiences the victory.

It is a book that everyone must read. It will enlighten us on what the power of love can accomplish. Read it, understand it, experience it, and declare it!

Reverend Wong Kim Kong, JMN

Reverend Wong Kim Kong, JMN, retired as the secretary general of the National Evangelical Christian Fellowship Malaysia. He was the founding chairman and former executive director of Malaysian CARE. He currently serves as adviser and consultant to about thirty organizations and churches, both locally and overseas.

FOREWORD

This book gives incredible insight to the challenging world of autism. If you are directly affected by having someone close to you living with autism, then you will identify with the raw, honest experiences related here. It will remind you that you are not alone in your very difficult journey and that there is always hope. In fact, hope and deep faith are the underpinning of this mother's long journey from a dark beginning to a bright future.

If you are unfamiliar about how autism affects the entire family, then this book will enlighten you to the huge challenges involved. It will increase your understanding of what must happen just to get through a 'normal' day, and it will doubtless increase your compassion for all living in this situation.

If you are a friend, pastoral carer, chaplain, or worker walking the journey alongside families in their autistic world, this book will give you keys for 'how to' and 'how not to'. It will teach you about life where 'abnormal' is 'normal', where criticism from ignorant people can cut to the core, where even surviving another day deserves a reward.

The author, Amelia, is very vulnerable in her journey as a mother of an autistic son. Her stories will make you smile, even chuckle ... and then grimace as you wonder how this family could survive day after day with such intense emotional, mental, spiritual, and physical challenges. Although sacrificing her own health and welfare in order to 'go to the ends of the world to ensure a better future for Aaron' (page 36), there was a pivotal day when the author rejected her depressed mindset and determined to adjust and succeed in what life had dished out to her. As husband and wife, they had to choose how to navigate and save their marriage from stresses which had the potential to tear them apart, demonstrating great wisdom and maturity.

I know this family personally. I did not know Aaron until he was seven years old, and I had no idea of the stresses that this family had lived with and overcome. They demonstrate the truth, that love and faith can eventually overcome all obstacles. This book describes the intense therapy and work by Aaron's family, which helped him develop to where he is today, a young man able to carve out his own life and celebrate many 'wins'.

As for Aaron himself, he is a delightful young man. We are allowed into the honesty of his struggles; his questions of 'Why me?'; his own spiritual development; his inspiring progress and determination to learn actions and behaviours that would make him appear 'normal', to fit in like everyone else. The result: 'he has publicly and officially lost his autism stigma' (page 153). People like myself, who have only entered his world in recent years, cannot identify the little boy in these pages with the delightful young man he is today.

So go ahead: plunge into this world of changing emotions, immense challenge, [and] endurance to the limits, [where you will] find hope, faith, love, wholeness, and victory.

Pastor Anne Iuliano

Pastor Anne Iuliano is the founder of Chaplaincy Australia, and she has been a pastor with the Australian Christian Churches for thirty-three years. She holds a master of arts in leadership, and she is a disaster and hospital chaplain. She is married to John (senior minister at North Shore Christian Centre, Chatswood, Sydney) and is mother to three adult children.

PREFACE

An introduction to the book
This book tells the story of my bittersweet experiences with my son, Aaron, who was born with autism. I hope that sharing my story will inspire parents and carers of children with disabilities, especially autism, to persevere in their difficult journeys. For the public, it is my hope that the book will raise awareness of the special needs of children with autism and accord them the empathy, support, and care that they need instead of criticism and condemnation born out of ignorance. Hopefully, it will also offer some helpful insight to the untrained childminders in their approach and treatment of children with autism, should any of them come under their care.

The title of this book, chosen by Aaron himself, is a true reflection of his thoughts and behavioural patterns prior to his 'rude awakening'. As he grew up into his teens, he realised he was not the one normal in this strange and confusing world. He aborted his original title, *Aaron with Autism and Aaron without Autism*, which he chose for the initial draft, completed four years ago, deciding it was now too childish and misleading.

The book is written in three parts.

The **first part** shares my biography and struggles with Aaron's disabilities.

The **second part** relates the episodes of Aaron's bizarre behaviour, depicting his various spectrums of autism. The story proper ends in part two, completed in the year 2010.

The **third part** was added in 2014 so that the story about Aaron is updated.

The **appendix,** consisting of frequently asked questions (FAQs), responds to the queries of interested parties and complements the areas that are not covered in the story.

The book is an attempt to give as comprehensive a picture as possible of the inner world of autism, as seen from the perspective of my son, Aaron. It is not written with any professional flair or knowledge of the subject. I am just an amateur storyteller sharing my experiences, as they were and are, and providing information I have learnt from my own research and seminars.

A Personal Testimony (a word of encouragement addressed to parents of children with autism)

You are not alone if you feel abandoned in your struggle, coping with the problems of raising an autistic child. I share your heartbeat, as I was there before. In fact, I was overwhelmed with stress to the point of exhaustion and at the same time gripped by a sense of helplessness and despair. Suffering the pain of hopes deferred, I even doubted God and wondered where He was in the midst of all my confusion and hurt. Facing a crisis of faith, I was irritated when Christians, clothed with well-intentioned spirituality, tried to assure me with the all-too-familiar clichés like 'Have more faith in God'. Said at the wrong time, at the wrong place, and by the wrong people, they only sounded hollow and lacking in empathy.

Yet I confess that it was precisely God that I sorely needed during the times when I found it the most difficult to trust Him. I would not have survived the throes of my journey had God not been there for me. The gloom of my joyless existence had turned me into a relentless cynic, disdainful and incredulous of anything good. It was a wonder that I did not let go of God – or rather that He did not let go of me. Though His presence did not always deliver me from my plight, He sustained me and did eventually restore order in my broken world.

God turned my situation around. Raising an autistic child is too daunting a task to go it alone. God was the bedrock of my wisdom and strength, and He can be yours too.

It is true that trusting God may or may not get us what we want or hope for. The sovereign God does not always pander to our wishes, move at our pace, and act according to our terms or preferences. Nevertheless, it makes sense for us to trust Him for the resources we need for ourselves and for our children. Even if we have strong faith in God, there are times when we face internal struggles beyond our ability to cope. It is important to be honest before God and to cry out to Him exactly how and what we feel, because He can handle what we can't.

My intention in writing this book is not to smack a plaster of hope and soothing balm over your pain with my success story. Nor am I promoting the power of optimism or positive thinking, chirping to the tune of 'Everything will be all right'.

Lest reading this book leaves you more confused with misplaced hopes, I wish to reiterate the obvious: every autistic child is unique and has his own special destiny, needs, and problems. Hence your child may respond differently to treatment and therapy from mine; what may work well for mine may not for yours, and vice-versa. Whatever road you take, there are no guarantees.

There is no shortcut or quick solution to the treatment or intervention program. It is easy to be influenced in this age of instant gratification, but truth be told, seeing our children through the learning and development programs is nothing short of a long haul. To quote Paul Collins, an American writer and parent of an autistic child, 'Autists are the ultimate square pegs, and the problem with pounding a square peg into a round hole is not that the hammering is hard work. It's that you're destroying the peg.' One of the most bitter pills to swallow is accepting the fact that a child is not normal and may only be able to master the most basic and elementary skills, even after days or months of hard work and drilling. Along the way, our energy levels are sapped and our patience tested. We wonder if a child will ever measure up, as we cannot see beyond the huge hurdles and obstacles that appear larger than life.

As typical mothers, the problem with us is that we are so focused on the final results of the therapies and programs that we tend to overlook the significance of the many baby steps needed to achieve them. Even when our children make it to their first milestones, we consider them too trifling and slow of a pace to rejoice in them. Yet it is vital that we learn to celebrate at the slightest sign of progress. Even if it takes ages before we see the smallest breakthrough, celebrate nevertheless! It is the only way to keep our heads up and our hopes sustained as we plod on positively, with the tiring journey ahead of us. Our children can become our trophies of divine grace. Sometimes breakthroughs come unexpectedly. So faint not and fight on, for tomorrow may come a song.

For the Christian parents, may I encourage you with a few verses of scripture verses that kept me going on the right track? When I was tempted to compare my child with another who was faring far better, I reminded myself of what the Lord said to Peter when he asked about John's destiny: 'If I want him to remain alive until I return, what is that to you? You must follow me' (John 21:22 NIV).

When I was going through my 'fiery furnace', I remembered the attitude of Shedrach, Meshach, and Abednego, 'If we are thrown into the fiery furnace, the God we serve is able to save us from it … … but even if he does not, we want you to know, O king, that we will not serve your gods or worship the image of gold you have set up." (Dan. 3:17-18)

My source of comfort has always been in Is. 61:3, that God is able to console those who mourn in Zion, to give them beauty for ashes. The 'ashes' for me had been the stress-strewn, obstacle-laden path of autism that I reluctantly trod with my son. From it, a thing of beauty gradually evolved as I began to see how God took the 'ashes' to shape me and to fill the niche He had planned in His purpose for me all along. It comes with a price tag of persistence and resilience.

I was inspired by a poem titled 'Thy Special Child'. To quote a few lines from the poem:

The angels said to the Lord above,
'This dear little child will need much love....
Please, Lord, find some parents for this child
Who'll do this good work as unto You.'

I resolved to be one of God's hand-picked parents to carry out His divine purpose for Aaron!

PART ONE
MY JOURNEY

CHAPTER 1

THE BEGINNING OF A LONG JOURNEY

The flurry of excitement that precedes, accompanies, and follows the birth of a baby is understandable, more so if the baby is the firstborn grandson of both sets of Asian parents. Thus Aaron's arrival into this world was a cause for celebration and exuberance. The cute little bundle of joy, endowed with sharp, well-defined features, was the centre of all the fuss and attention. However, it seemed that he was born with an innate revulsion for attention right from birth. He overtly resisted any fuss over him and yelled his lungs out at the slightest provocation. Once upset, he was not easily pacified.

After the initial euphoria over Aaron's birth subsided and eventually evaporated, the stark reality of being hemmed in by a very difficult-to-please baby sank in. I became a bundle of nerves, trying to cope with his incessant cries and demands. Being a first-time mother, I was perplexed about a number of things. Was he crying because my breast milk was too diluted or had he had too much or too little to drink? Did I eat the wrong confinement food, perhaps with too much ginger? Was it his chronic colic or was I just lacking in mothering skills? The many questions that ran through my mind threw me into utter confusion. I found myself attending to him 24/7, constantly breastfeeding him, carrying him, coaxing him to sleep, changing him, washing him, and doing everything I could to earn the peace and rest I sorely needed. Thanks to Aaron's poor adaptation to this world right from the start of his life, I was drained to my last ounce of energy.

Hardly did I realize that post-partum blues and depression hit me in the first month. I became extremely sensitive to any remark made about Aaron or me, even if it was a good well-intentioned advice or suggestion. I was at the end of myself, accentuated by constant migraines and sleep deprivation. It was no help that I had a problem getting back to sleep after attending to Aaron, especially at night. I was increasingly agitated, despondent, anxious, and tensed up. My frequent mood swings ran counter to my normal cheerful, radiant self. My personality went through a drastic turnover. In my morose and downcast state, I snapped at anything and anyone, with the one closest to me, my husband, getting the full brunt of it. I was in a predicament; much as I needed help, I turned down my husband's offer to relieve me for some nights. I wanted him to focus on his rising career, and knowing that he was already tired out from frequent night calls, I had no heart to burden him with Aaron's problems. Besides, there was little anyone else could do, as I was breastfeeding and Aaron needed only me to attend to him. It gave me little option but to plod on, by God's grace.

Aaron became abnormally dependent on me. The moment he opened his eyes, I had to be there for him. By the time he was ten to twelve months old, he started developing habits that were nearly impossible to break. He had to feel my left wrist and wristwatch each time he drifted in and out of sleep. It had become such a compulsive routine to him that I had to place my left hand within his reach every night so that he could dose off again after feeling my wrist and the watch. The problem was, even if Aaron got back to sleep, I could not do so once he woke me up. Aaron's obsessive habit contributed to and perpetuated my condition of sleep deprivation. I was at my wits' end as to how the habit could be broken, not just for Aaron's sake but more so for mine.

One night I asked my dad to relieve me after Aaron had fallen asleep. He tried putting on my wristwatch and stretching out his hand the way I usually did. My plan for salvaging some sleep backfired miserably, and I wound up losing my sleep altogether that night. Aaron just could not be tricked; when he woke up, he could sense that it was not my hand, so he started screaming in the middle of the night. I had little choice but to resume my place in seeing to him. He eventually calmed down and drifted off to sleep again, but I was too wide awake to return to sleep.

His evident inflexibility was also seen in other ways. The lullaby from a CD which I used to lull him to sleep became an obsession to him, and he simply could not sleep without listening to it. It had to be played – at times, replayed repeatedly – until he fell asleep, or he would be greatly distressed.

At mealtimes, he had to watch the same video from *Veggie Tales*, and it had to be repeated until he had finished his meal. Once he got used to anything, he adhered rigidly to the routine. The slightest deviation would unsettle him altogether and drive him into a rage.

He loved repetition, be it a song, a show, or an action. The action he enjoyed repeating most was spinning around.

Even with many rounds, he didn't seem to get dizzy. Instead, he enjoyed the sensation so much that he seemed to be on an ecstatic high. He would not stop unless he was distracted by something fascinating.

When he started crawling at nine months, I noticed that he never put anything into his mouth the way other children did. Whenever he was given food to eat, including biscuits that he liked, he would only throw it away. I dismissed my concern about it, thinking that he was not too interested in food, even though he would gladly eat the same food if someone fed it to him. I was confused. Little did I realize that it was not a natural instinct for him to use his hands to put food into his mouth.

When he grew to be a toddler, he appeared to have a strange passion for things that were not typical of toddlers his age. He was fascinated with signage, like traffic signs and even drab signboards. In the supermarkets, he would grab at any of the price tags that were within his reach. Woe betide us if we should be in a hurry and pass by any traffic signs or signboards! We would not be able to proceed from there. Aaron would insist that we remained there for him to gaze at the signage from different angles. His rage knew no bounds if we would forcefully drag him away from it. To avoid any commotion, especially in public places, we often ended up complying with his wishes. Looking peevishly foolish, we would stand together with Aaron, rooted before or below a meaningless signboard, just staring at it aimlessly until he was satisfied. Fortunately, it usually didn't stretch beyond a few minutes.

Aaron still obsessed with traffic signs at age four

For the first three years after Aaron was born, we were apprehensive about going on vacation, as Aaron was unable to sleep anywhere else except on his own bed. He was not at all adaptable to any kind of change, especially sleeping on a strange bed without the familiar surroundings and the things in the room which were his security. We decided to take a much-needed short holiday in Lake Macquarie, not far from Sydney. He was uneasy and ready to go home. I had to coax and distract him with his favourite pursuits. At night, I had to lie with him, as he had to keep touching my left wrist and watch, essentially his security blanket, before he finally fell asleep.

The next morning would see Aaron exploring every room of the apartment we stayed in, touching the things he'd fancied on the first day we arrived. He particularly enjoyed the tactile sensation of soft materials, especially carpet. Whatever he did would become his daily ritual for the following days. He would perform his routine rounds by going to the rooms in the same sequence and going to the same spots and touching the same things each time.

From the time he was very young I could tell that Aaron was unlike other children in his behaviour. He would not use his finger to point at anything. Instead, he would just drag my hand and use it to obtain a desired item, as he had no other form of communication. Puzzled by his weird behaviour, I chose to think positively. As a mother with no knowledge of 'autism' in my vocabulary, my wildest dream was that he belonged to a special genre of smart kids, a breed that could possibly have the potential and making of the eccentric and unconventional Einsteins. An impossible dream, perhaps, but the vision was good for my soul. It gave me hope and encouragement that my sacrifice would pay off in the end.

CHAPTER 2

AN UNEXPECTED GIFT

My second pregnancy was not planned. Coping with Aaron's demands and aggressive behaviour was itself quite a nightmare; having another child was the furthest from my rational mind. In hindsight, having a sibling close to Aaron's age was the best thing that had ever happened to him. I thanked God that in His wisdom, He overruled our natural tendency to pander to human reasoning and rationale. In this case, the long-term gain, in exchange for the short-term pain, was God's creative way of seeing Aaron through the process of his development and growth in a normal environment.

The pregnancy went smoothly, without any eventful incident. However, by the last stage of my pregnancy, I was getting a little too heavy and could hardly walk without pain. Thankfully, my parents had arrived earlier from Malaysia to help me.

Despite my tummy growing bigger by the day, Aaron was quite oblivious to what was happening. I prayed hard that he would not be traumatised when the time came for my delivery, and I wondered if he could take to the temporary separation during the period. Weeks before that, we tried to prepare him by letting him spend more and more time away from me, at his paternal grandparents' house. His grandparents would see to him during that time.

The day came when baby Alysha was born. Unfortunately, I had suffered the side effects of the epidural and needed to have complete bed rest for a few days after the birth due to acute migraines.

After a week, I was still not well enough to welcome Aaron home, but I visited Aaron in my in-laws' home. I wondered how Aaron would react to me after a week of 'abandonment'. When I entered the house, I called out to him affectionately, but he did not acknowledge me. There was an uncomfortable silence. It was as if he needed time to recognize me and to adjust to me, his primary caregiver, all over again. I could not fathom what was going through his mind or read the reason for his unresponsiveness. Perhaps he needed time to process the hurt and rejection after suffering a short period of separation. He obviously needed assurance before he could be 'normal' in his relationship with me again. I visited him a few times before he gradually responded to me. His grandparents brought him home after a few weeks with them.

Aaron showed absolutely no tenderness or feelings for his baby sister. He wasn't even interested in looking at her. He showed not the slightest inkling of understanding as to who this little stranger was, and he was totally indifferent to her. Possibly in his mind, baby Alysha was just a toy. When he did pay attention to her, he had no qualms about pinching her eyes, nose, and ears. It was obvious that he didn't welcome the little 'intruder' into his family. He demonstrated his displeasure by protesting and kicking a big fuss whenever I held his baby sister. He was aggressive in wanting to monopolize me for himself. I always had to distract him with things he enjoyed doing so that I could attend to his sister.

Aaron had to be trained to love and hug his sister, but it was not easy or natural with him. He had to be chided ever so often for pushing and shoving her away, small and helpless as she was. We had to be extremely vigilant lest he attack the poor baby and injure her. Perhaps all he saw was a little nuisance or rival who had usurped his right to have the full attention of his mother.

It was far from easy for me to cope with both Aaron and the baby. I am thankful for my parents, who stayed on for six months to help during the trying period. After they left, the daily grind took a toll on me, despite my in-laws stepping in every now and then to help.

CHAPTER 3

THE DIAGNOSIS

E ngaging in healthy self-talk did at times help to allay my deepest fears and anxieties. At the height of Aaron's impossible behaviour, I used to tell myself that it was a temporary phase, typical of children going through the stage of the terrible twos.

Then one day an article caught my attention, striking a deep sense of foreboding in my heart. The description in the article was about a mum relating her teenage son's experience with autism. The son did not like being touched and avoided looking at people's expressions because they confused him. He loved things to be in order, and he would scream on the road each time he could not see beyond the horizon where the road would end. The description struck a deep chord in my heart, as it appeared to be an exact replica of Aaron's behaviour. The striking and uncanny resemblance disturbed me mentally and emotionally, though my defensive mindset chose to reject any possibility that my son was anything but normal. Even though I hardly understood what autism really meant at that juncture, I kept the apprehensive doubt to myself. Little did I realize that it was God preparing me for what was to come. While I was eager to have Aaron tested immediately by a paediatrician – hoping that she would confirm that my fears were unfounded – I was told to wait until Aaron was three before any diagnosis could be made.

The day after his third birthday, we made an appointment with the paediatrician. On arriving at the clinic, Aaron avoided eye contact and ignored the paediatrician when she spoke to him. After observing him for a while, she noticed that he did not pick up any toy in the room and just went to a corner by himself. He made some incoherent sounds and was obviously feeling a little distressed. The paediatrician asked questions – for example, whether Aaron had symptoms, such as a liking for alphabets and numbers, repetitive behaviour, and a dislike for social settings with many people. When I affirmed that Aaron displayed all the symptoms that she mentioned, her diagnosis was that Aaron had classic autism. Her diagnosis was based on the minimum number of criteria that matched Aaron's behaviour.

For a moment, I was numb when the paediatrician confirmed his medical condition, even though I was half expecting it. My heart sank with the knowledge that Aaron really did have a disability syndrome that was irreversible. Yet I was strangely relieved that I at last understood the reason for Aaron's aggressiveness and obsessive-compulsive behaviour which was so unlike other children. I also felt relieved that Aaron's behaviour – which appeared like that of an incorrigible spoilt brat – was not equated to my failure in disciplining him as a mother. I had borne the anguish of many insensitive, insidious, and insinuating remarks about Aaron's unacceptable behaviour and the implication of my incompetence as a mother. When those closest to me made such remarks, the emotional pain was deep. As I struggled with the knowledge, I came to the point of resignation that I was inadequate. Though angry and irritated at times, I knew I could not blame anyone for making those insensitive and hurtful comments, however well intended. After all, the misconstrued perception was made out of ignorance and from the perspective of the norm. Who would ever expect Aaron to be different and to be a 'special' child?

I plucked myself up very quickly. I felt the pressure to act immediately after being told that intervention had to be started early, as it would not be effective after he turned six. The pragmatic side of me seemed to triumph over the melancholy; there was just no time for denial and languishing over past hurts and regrets. Neither should I wallow in my grief and despair. Much had to be done so that Aaron could get into an early intervention program without any delay. The quicker Aaron had access to intervention, the better his prospects of improving. The urgency of it drove me to research desperately on autism through the Internet and through the books available in the library. I also found out about the programs available for autistic children. All of a sudden, I seemed to be bombarded with the pressure of endless things that needed to be done. I needed to apply quickly to get Aaron enrolled in the right schools. I also got in touch with people who had some knowledge about autism, seeking the right advice.

In the midst of it all, I could not help being plagued with the nagging doubts and anxieties about Aaron's future. Would he be accepted into any of the programs? Would he be able to talk? Was there any way out for him?

The first school my husband and I applied to for Aaron was Giant Steps, one of the two privately funded schools for autistic students in Sydney. To my horror, the waiting list for the school was unexpectedly long. There were only three spots for over fifty applicants on the waiting list. Aaron was just one among the many who were autistic. Our hopes that he could ever stand a chance of getting in were dashed to the ground. Not surprisingly, our first application for Aaron was rejected.

We then tried the public schools. We were grateful for the one-day-a-week program that Aaron would have from 9.45 a.m. to 2 p.m., October to December 2001.

At the same time, we also started seeking out private therapists. Aaron went under the tutelage of an occupational therapist and a speech therapist. At the advice of the therapists, we submitted a second application to Giant Steps. With the referral of Aaron's occupational therapist, we were successful in getting him enrolled this time! At the point when my despondency had almost hit rock bottom, God did indeed graciously intervene and answer our prayers. We readily agreed to the condition of helping in fundraising events for the school every year. Though it meant hard work, it was really a small price to pay in exchange for the prize of being accepted into a good school for autistic children.

This was only the beginning of good news. Unexpectedly, Aaron was also accepted into the Star Program, a project sponsored by Macquarie University's Special Education unit. It was an experimental program where special needs children were placed in a normal preschool. There were special needs specialists to train the children on fine motor skills and school preparation skills (for example, sitting down in class, taking turns, and self-help) for three hours a day. The other three hours were aimed at training the special needs children to socialise with normal children. The Star Program was conducted as a research program to gauge the effectiveness of placing a special needs program in a normal preschool setting. It was also aimed at gauging whether the program would help in transitioning the special needs children into normal schools.

My excitement was short-lived. The days for the two schools clashed, and we were faced with the dilemma of which school to place Aaron in. We could not have the best of both worlds. It was a tough decision to make, as each program had its strengths and benefits. At the preschool, Aaron would have an opportunity to integrate with normal children, but he also needed the therapies designed for autistic children that were available at Giant Steps.

While we were praying for the right decision, a miracle happened. He was promoted to the advanced class in Giant Steps. As the advanced class fell on Wednesdays, Thursdays, and Fridays, that meant that Aaron was free to attend the preschool program, which fell on Mondays and Tuesdays. If that was not the favour of God, I don't know what was!

I was prepared to take on the challenge of the whole package, which involved raising funds for both the schools. I thought of the pressure of juggling all of Aaron's programs, therapies, home responsibilities, fundraising activities into my tight schedule, but nothing deterred me. I would go to the ends of the world to ensure a better future for Aaron. I believed in God's infinite strength and resources to see me through. It was an opportunity that was hard to come by, and I was prepared to strive, whatever the cost, in order to give Aaron the very best, even if it meant sapping the last ounce of energy out of me. My confidence was in God's resources, not mine.

CHAPTER 4

ALMOST CAVING IN TO PRESSURE

I was thankful that Aaron had a good head start immediately after his diagnosis at three and a half years of age. The intervention programs provided by the two schools that he attended were excellent.

Nevertheless, I had to face the stark reality of coping with the extra responsibilities that came along with them. Stretching myself to the limit, I wondered sometimes if I could withstand the strain for long. Day by day, I seemed to be hanging on to my last reserves of strength. The whole package was much more demanding and stressful than I had thought. However bright the sun might be shining outside, I got up each morning consumed with a pervasive, foreboding sense of darkness in my mind and soul, with nothing to look forward to each day. It robbed me of whatever little confidence and courage I had to face the strain and challenges ahead.

To the world outside, I looked the picture of strength and composure, one who viewed the jam-packed panorama of my life with quiet confidence. However, the stoic impregnable demeanour belied the real self that was cracking under pressure. It was as if I were wearing a mask and living in a world of pretence, putting on a forced wry smile and managing a well-controlled front. But beneath the facade was the real me, on the verge of a breakdown and crumbling under the weight of an endless cycle of responsibilities and cares.

Perhaps I might have coped better if I did not have to put up with the additional pressure of Aaron's tantrums. I had to plan everything 'right' to ensure that Aaron would not be provoked. This kept me on tenterhooks for the most part of the day, as I could never be too sure when the unanticipated or unpredictable would happen. Once his tantrum, which could last for hours, was triggered, not only were my scheduled plans for the day disrupted, but my whole day would be more or less ruined. Aaron alone could take up all my time, but I also had to care for Alysha. My husband also needed his fair share of support and encouragement from me as he was making inroads into his career. My multifaceted responsibilities seemed to be tearing me apart and affecting my health. My head felt as if it was exploding at times; the pressure and the constant coping with the insurmountable demands of each day manifested in constant migraines, giddy spells, and sleepless nights. One thing led to another. Being weak physically, I was prone to occasional flu infections, especially during the winter months. It was worse when my whole family succumbed to the flu virus one by one and needed even more of my attention and care.

Tension became an integral part of my life. As a parent to Aaron, I was required to attend meetings regularly in his schools and be involved in such fund-raising activities as selling dinner tickets, chocolates, Entertainment Books (books with discount coupons to popular eateries and so forth), and organising shopping trips to factory outlets. With my limited circle of friends who would oblige by purchasing the things I promoted, I had to contend with ways and means to meet the target. I needed time for all of these projects and activities, and time was my greatest constraint. Fortunately, a few of my close friends, knowing my plight, helped by promoting the products for me.

In between a hectic schedule, I taught music lessons two afternoons a week; my in-laws would look after the children. The normal daily routine filled up all my time, and I felt as if I hardly had much time to breathe. As I tried to muster enough energy to see myself through each day, I seemed bereft of any joy or meaning in life. I had to fight the miasma of hopelessness that was gradually gripping me. There were two occasions when I wanted to throw in the towel. It was too much for me to handle. When my emotions reached rock bottom, I even cried out to God to take me home to be with Him. I remember wanting to drive my car, with Aaron in it, into a ditch or a dam to drown ourselves. I wanted to end it all. It was in those moments of utter fuzziness and confusion in my mind that God restrained me and gave me thoughts from the Bible. They jolted me out of my irrational, insane moments. I could literally feel an external hug that was so tight that I just had to let go and surrender completely. It was God's arms of love embracing me.

Yet despite experiencing God's hug, I was still not set free from my negative state of mind, for I could hardly see any sign of Aaron's progress, especially in his behaviour. His ability to pick up skills also seemed to be alarmingly slow. It was sheer craziness and frustration to me, having to teach Aaron the same elementary skills repeatedly in different situations. For example, when I taught him to close the door gently and not to slam it, he only did so for that particular door and not for any other door. Similarly, when he was taught to tie a bow with his shoelace, he could not understand that the same skill could be applied to a thread, string, or a rope. Even when he was taught to say hello to somebody, he had to be prompted to use the same greeting each time for any other person. It was not, in his mind, a blanket social greeting for everyone. He could not generalise and apply any simple instruction or skill learnt across multiple settings, environments, and people. His deficiency added to my overwhelming stress each day.

The future seemed uncertain and bleak. I wondered whether my sacrifice would count for anything. Perhaps as insulation to my frayed nerves, I began to grow inured to Aaron's screams and tantrums, which were a daily ordeal. At times, when I was completely drained of energy, I would appear totally heartless, unresponsive, and deaf to Aaron's screams for my attention.

One evening when my husband arrived home, instead of a haven of peace and rest after a hard day's work, the home was in disarray, with Aaron screaming at the top of his voice in the background. The tension-charged environment was the last thing he needed greeting him. He tried to attend to Aaron immediately, but his attempt only caused Aaron's screams to escalate further. After some time, my husband was also reaching the limit of his tolerance, overwhelmed by his own sense of helplessness. He was torn between his earnestness in wanting to give me some form of relief and his helplessness in handling the situation. The stress at work, culminated by his anxiety in preparing for his coming specialist examination, was further aggravated by the tension at home. His threshold for tolerance and patience was wearing thin.

On my part, I had already spent half an hour or more wiping Aaron's tears. It didn't appear to have any effect in helping him to stop crying. To carry on would be meaningless, especially when there were many urgent things that needed to be done. I had to ignore him and leave him to his own devices. He could not tolerate the sensation of his tears streaming slowly down his face, and the more upset he got, the more the tears flowed. A vicious cycle, no human had the means of stopping it. The only way those tumultuous times could end naturally was through sheer exhaustion due to his non-stop crying.

My irritability had me in a most vulnerable state, built up through seemingly endless days of toil and strain. It just needed the slightest trigger to cause me to explode. Much as I understood that my husband had a legitimate reason to stay longer hours away from home to prepare for his specialist examination, I was harbouring repressed anger that he was selfishly leaving the burden at home entirely to me and was not lending the emotional support that I needed so desperately.

One particular day, we were both stretched to the point of losing control. It happened over such a minor incident. Despite Aaron's tantrum, my husband was not prepared to abort the plan he had made for us to meet up with some friends for recreation. Being worn out physically and emotionally, I was in no mood for an outing. I couldn't help snapping angrily at him when he insisted that we needed that break, with or without Aaron's tantrum. Tempers flared up, and heated arguments ensued. Signs of marital concerns began to loom in our relationship.

It was a wake-up call in our marriage. Fortunately, the strong foundation of God and love in our relationship safeguarded it from being dented irretrievably. We took charge of ourselves and the situation and decided to have our time out to talk through the many issues. We did not allow our pent-up emotions to get the better of us. We refrained from stubbornly insisting on our own rights, interests, and decisions for the nobler cause of guarding the sanctity of our covenanted marital relationship.

We aired feelings, hurts, and grievances openly. We realized that we were both guilty of allowing stress and frustration to affect our relationship adversely. We worked through our differences and were able to arrive at a mutual understanding and a more mature level of love in our relationship.

God alerted us early that the oft-repeated patterns of marital wear and tear, the web of push and pull and power play, were the common factors for cracks and breakups in relationships, especially for couples with autistic children. Very often the multifaceted problems related to an autistic child, such as aggressive behaviour, a special diet, costly therapies, and financial constraint, can create a climate ripe for marital conflict. The discord nearly always stem from an intense argument as to who is doing more or bearing a greater load. Both may have an exhausting day, he at work and she having to cope with the tantrums of the autistic child at home. Perhaps unintentionally, the wife may treat her husband as a convenient outlet for her frustration and nagging complaints. As for the husband, he may also be physically and emotionally wiped out. If his threshold of tolerance and patience is overstretched, dissatisfaction in the relationship will naturally set in. This will give rise to more squabbles and angst-ridden verbal outbursts. If not addressed early, it will lead to irreparable damage to the marriage relationship.

We thank God that He protected our marriage relationship as we leaned on His strength during the times when we had little to give to each other.

In the meantime, my husband could perceive that I was becoming more and more of a social recluse and a shut-in, and he was truly concerned. My behaviour and attitude were reflecting that I had lost all enthusiasm for life. He felt that I was all bottled up inside and needed an outlet or a break. He tried hard to arrange for a few of my close friends to take me out, but it was a madcap attempt, quite out of line with my mental state at that time. I was too exhausted and dispirited for any kind of social activity or getaway.

Realizing that it could be the onset of depression, I had to pull myself out of it consciously. With God's help, I was able to forge good friendships with the mothers of Aaron's friends in the same school. We shared similar needs and common problems; thus we were able to empathize and lend support to one another. It was certainly a helpful outlet and release for me.

We formed a good support group for one another. We were able to have tea together and attend some useful courses for mothers of autistic children. The courses were indeed helpful in educating us and equipping us to understand and, at the same time, help our children more effectively. We shared encouraging counsel, tips, and strategies, and my confidence in handling the problems related to autism was built up.

In one of the courses, an essay titled 'Welcome to Holland' (by Emily Perl Kingsley, available on the Internet) was read, and many of us were moved to tears after hearing it. The author was a mother of a disabled child, and we were able to identify with what she portrayed.

Personally, the essay touched the core of my heart as it beautifully and inoffensively urged me to come to terms with the reality of the unexpected, unwarranted, and unjustifiable position as a mother of an autistic child. I felt encouraged to respond positively by taking up the challenge to become the best mother for my child. The essay, written by one who'd shared the same heartbeat and plodded through a similar rough journey, had a deep impact on me. It made me rethink my role positively.

I saw myself as one who had made every preparation to land in Venice. I had looked forward to experiencing the romance of sailing in gondolas and the thrill of speaking the Italian language. I had boarded a plane and expected to land at my destination, but I found myself landing in Holland instead, a land of windmills, with apparently nothing exciting to look forward to. I had not mentally and emotionally opted or prepared myself for that place. What was I to do in such a predicament?

The poem was a catalyst in propelling me toward a more constructive and positive world view of life. As if arriving at a watershed, a defining decisive moment, I could even echo, with a sudden surge of triumph, the speech of Shakespeare's *Julius Caesar*: 'I came. I saw. I conquered.' My victory was not in new territories but in my new mindset. I conquered my hitherto narrow, disgruntled perspective and so set the stage for a greater conquest – the discovery of the wonder and beauty of 'Holland', where I had landed.

I needed to cease daydreaming about what I would have enjoyed had I landed in Venice as originally planned as well as quit spending the rest of the time lamenting my landing in Holland. Instead, I could welcome the unexpected destination as a challenge in my voyage and discover new treasures that Holland had to offer. To move on meant taking decisive steps in picking up the pieces and re-orientating myself to learning a brand-new language and culture. In so doing, I would discover a new world of fresh opportunities open and waiting for me.

Infused with fresh hope, courage, and expectancy, I saw a turning point in my life. I no longer saw myself immersed in the sea of burdens and cares. Putting aside all negative vibes, discouragement, and a despondent attitude, I felt the surge of God's overcoming spirit upon me. At last, a glimmer of light had appeared at the end of the tunnel, and it has beamed brighter and brighter ever since.

CHAPTER 5

THE BREAKING OF DAWN

The vista of endless days fraught with disappointment, fatigue, and stress drew to a close after Aaron turned five. The first breakthrough came after he learnt to communicate using picture cards instead of words. His screaming and tantrums lessened, and his behaviour naturally improved through his ability to make himself understood. Gradually, he learnt to read and understand sentences, leading to his marked progress in social skills. With a better grasp of language, he was able to follow and obey clear instructions. Visible signs of his progress were seen in every area of his development, not just in his behaviour, speech, and social skills but also in his gross motor skills. He was also growing to be more independent and manageable.

I was gradually more at peace and in control of myself and life as a whole. Aaron's sister, Alysha, had overcome her obstinate terrible twos phase and was less demanding of my attention. My husband was also more settled and established in his career as a consultant anaesthetist.

Being more financially stable, we decided to move from our town house to a bigger bungalow with a sizeable garden for the children to romp around. But our major concern was whether it was too traumatic a move for Aaron to handle. Knowing how routine-bound and resistant he was to any form of change, however minor, we were filled with a sense of uneasiness and apprehension. A major move to an unfamiliar place with a completely new surrounding might just throw him off kilter. The town house was the place associated with his growing-up years and to which he had grown much attached. We anticipated and feared the worst, that the adverse effect might leave an indelible mark on his anxiety syndrome.

Preparation for the move was vital for Aaron. His therapists took on the task to prepare him mentally and emotionally for the drastic change of place. It took them two months. They went over to the new home, took many pictures, and created a social story to help him understand the move and the reasons for doing so. This helped him to cope with the concept. His therapists then took him countless times to the new place to familiarise him with the house. He ran in the garden and physically touched the new house. They also prepared him by taking him through the route from the new house to school so that he would be used to it when the time came.

In the old house, Aaron slept with his sister and me in the same room on two mattresses. With the change of a new house, the therapists also prepared him for a new sleeping arrangement, where he would sleep with his sister in one bedroom whilst his mum would sleep with his dad in another bedroom. The therapists essentially helped him understand the benefits of the new house compared to the old. He needed time to process the change and become conditioned to accept the new unfamiliar ground that we were shifting to.

When the day drew near, we sensed that he was growing increasingly sombre and reticent. He obviously understood what was happening, and I believed he was getting himself psyched up for the move. He needed the time to mourn over the place that he was going to miss and leave behind. He spent much time alone in his room. We were too busy packing to check on what he was really doing.

When the day finally arrived, we were pleasantly surprised that his demeanour and behaviour were far from what we had expected. He seemed to have already grieved over the situation and was mentally prepared for the big move. He sheepishly bid goodbye to the old house as we drove away from it. He did not turn back to gaze at it longingly or sentimentally for the last time. In fact, he refused to look at it again. He had programmed his mind for the change, even though it must have been hard and painful for him at first. For months after that, he would intentionally avoid looking in the direction of the old house each time we passed by it. It was his way of coping with his sense of loss.

The old house was well shaded by surrounding trees and was cold, dark, and gloomy, especially in winter. The new house, by contrast, had a bright and cheery look. It was as if the greater accessibility to sunlight had a magical effect in lifting the veil of gloom that used to loom ominously in the surroundings. The general well-being and morale of the family seemed to be in tandem with the invariable change of environment.

Aaron seemed happier too. There was a large compound for him and his sister to run around and play in; there was more space in the house for them to play with their toys and games, and also more shelves and cupboards to store their favourite books.

Amelia Chin

My personality also gradually evolved from being a cold, sullen, and stoic self to a more joyful, energetic, and enthusiastic person who had gone through almost a full cycle. Just like the seasons, winter had passed and spring had come. Unknowingly, I had allowed the 'texture' of the seasons to seep through the pores of each fibre in my personality traits.

Looking back, I recall words of encouragement that I heard during my pregnancy and while I was going through those difficult days. At that time, I discarded them as being unreal, irrelevant, and even impossible, for I could not see the dimmest light of their truth during those trying times. All I saw was the darkness of my own soul. Even though devout men of God had uttered the encouraging words, I confess that I glossed over them as comforting Christian platitudes that did not amount to much.

One of them told me during my pregnancy that my unborn son was a very blessed child. Another one mentioned that God had reminded him about the story of Elisha, the Shunammite woman, and her son (2 Kin. 4:8–37) when he interceded in prayer for Aaron and me. He advised me to meditate prayerfully on the story together with the verse in Rom. 4:17. He also reminded me not to forget 'practising the presence of God' in my life. I saw no meaningful correlation between my situation and that of the Shunammite woman in the story; it only left me in a state where I was more baffled than comforted.

Today I perceive the story differently; I see it as God's prophetic word to me, to inspire hope in me. Just as the servant of God met the Shunammite woman's problem of barrenness, so would God meet the barrenness and sense of helplessness in my soul as I sought Him. When Aaron was diagnosed with autism, it was like an impasse, a dead situation that did not auger well for the future. However, just as life was restored to the 'dead' boy in the story, so would God restore 'life' to Aaron's situation. The fulfilment of this was incumbent upon my faithfulness and in cultivating the presence of God in my life.

I am grateful that despite my negative outlook, God's hand was and still is upon Aaron. His work of restoration is a lifelong process. Though Aaron may not totally overcome all his limitations and be 'healed' of autism, he has come a long way. I couldn't have asked for more. I have confidence that when he grows up, he will find his niche in society, where his special gifts and talents will be tapped for a wonderful purpose and vocation that God has in store for him.

PART TWO

DRAMATIC EPISODES RELATING TO SPECTRUMS OF AUTISM

CHAPTER 6

INSATIABLE OBSESSIONS AND COMPULSIVE NEED FOR SET PATTERNS

(a) Traffic Signs

When Aaron was between three to five years of age, looking after him was a real nightmare. It is natural for every parent to put up with the occasional shrill whining of a young child and the high-pitched screams that pierce the eardrums, but for me it had been almost like a daily grind. The good, restful, and peaceful days were rare and far in between. Just when my taut nerves were taking a well-deserved rest, the unexpected would always trigger the next raging episode. Many of Aaron's temper tantrums were associated with his obsessions with signage. He had a peculiar penchant for traffic signs.

One evening Aaron was watching *The Hooley Dooleys* on TV. He was so absorbed with it that I found the perfect opportunity to slip away quietly for a quick bath upstairs. I didn't have the luxury of going to the bathroom at leisure, for I had to be constantly by his side or at least not out of his sight. No one, not his grandparents nor even his dad, could take my place.

The moment I went upstairs, I heard his sharp shrill cry. I thought it was his usual fuss about my absence, but this time it was far more intense. He was protesting vehemently about something that had happened.

I rushed downstairs, only to realize that the show had his favourite GIVE WAY sign in a background scene and it disappeared in the next scene. He demanded to see the GIVE WAY sign again. He could not understand that a replay of a TV show was impossible. It was a waste of time trying to explain it to him. He was beyond reason, and nothing could pacify him or take its place. A tiny insignificant scene sparked off Aaron's irrational behaviour and exasperation that evening. He only stopped crying when he finally fell asleep from exhaustion.

Seeing Aaron's passion for traffic signs, his granddad indulged him with some miniature cardboard ones which he painstakingly made with great accuracy. These signs were glued on to straws, and they were soon littered all over the house. As the GIVE WAY sign was Aaron's favourite, he played with it day and night. It became something he was so attached to that he could not live without it.

Aaron with his traffic signs;
note his favourite GIVE WAY sign

However, through long and frequent usage and normal wear and tear, the demise of his idol became imminent; the print started to fade in colour, and the sign began to tear. The day came when part of it peeled off. His dad and I did everything we could to glue back the torn part and to make it look as original as possible. But to Aaron, it was not the same. We even made a coloured computer printout of it, but even that was not acceptable. We ran out of ideas and resources to know what to do. To Aaron, he had lost something very precious, and nothing could stop his moaning, wailing, and yelling for hours. We had to put up with what we believe was the grieving period for his loss. What initially had brought him so much fun and excitement turned out to be a source of pain and trauma.

Sometime later, his granddad decided to make traffic signs mounted on wooden rods and bases. These were more solid compared to the earlier signs glued on to with straws. As expected, they again became Aaron's favourite pastime and absorbing hobby. He visualized in his mind the house as a road map or a little town, and he positioned the different signs at the various strategic places. The whole house became like a fantasy land strewn with traffic signs. His pleasure became everyone else's pain. We had to be very careful where we treaded. We didn't have the liberty to walk freely around the house anymore. We had to take great care not to step on, trip over, or displace any of the traffic signs that Aaron laid out meticulously and strategically. More so for me! Aaron even expected me to follow a particular circuitous route to go to the toilet in order to avoid violating any traffic rules in the land of his imagination. The slightest slip meant chaos and enduring another round of Aaron's long-drawn-out tantrum.

Realizing that the GIVE WAY sign had become Aaron's indispensable possession, duplicates were made of it, but he liked only one of them in particular. It became like his security blanket, which he would take with him wherever he went, even to the shopping malls.

I had to be extra vigilant lest he drop it and cause an uncontrollable outburst. Despite the extra care taken, the inevitable happened one day in a shopping centre. In one of the supermarkets, he got so distracted by a toy he liked that the GIVE WAY sign slipped out of his hand unnoticed by anyone. He was holding on to the toy. By the time we were about to line up at the payment counter, he suddenly realized that his GIVE WAY sign was not in his hand. He screamed, and I panicked. I tried giving him the duplicate which I had in my bag, but he could recognize that it was a different one. He demanded to have back the lost one immediately. As embarrassment would have it, his persistent raving and screaming soon attracted the disapproving stares of the people around us. Realizing the gravity of the situation, my parents, who were with me at that time, immediately rushed back to the different parts of the shopping centre that we had been to in order to look for the lost treasure. Meanwhile, I had to put up with the hard frowns of some of the older women around, which spoke the message loud and clear: 'For goodness' sake, shut up your kid!'

I thanked the Lord that the ordeal only lasted for about fifteen minutes. My dad found the sign in an obscure corner of the supermarket and retrieved it. Aaron immediately stopped yelling and gazed gleefully at his lost possession, now found. Having scrutinized and examined it carefully to ensure that it was the right one, he held on to it tightly and started smiling again.

But the nightmare was far from over. As we were heading towards the payment counter, I realized, to my dismay, that the express counter was closed. The express counter was the one we used the first time we came to the supermarket. Since then, Aaron had programmed in his mind that we should only use that counter. That became his norm and routine. I had to conform to it at all cost, even to the extent of limiting my purchases to less than eight items each time so that I was 'qualified' to use the express counter. Though the express counter was closed, we still had to use the same route to it, which meant passing through the pets' aisle which was rather smelly. In haste, we had used it the first time, as it was the shortcut to the express counter, so it became *the* route for Aaron. To any right-thinking person, using that route would be the most insensible thing to do, but with Aaron any other route was non-negotiable.

Hoping against hope that he would be more accommodating that day, I took my chance in queuing up at the normal counter.

He started whinging, and before long he was forcefully wriggling out of his pram and squealing in protest. I decided immediately to make a quick exit before he got out of control, rolling and screaming unashamedly on the floor as he had done before. I left the trolley behind, packed with all the groceries I'd needed that day. At least I escaped another round of commotion, coupled with the unsympathetic glares of the women around me. Though the shopping spree turned out to be a total fiasco, I left feeling glad that I acted in time to prevent another full-blown tantrum. Ever since that episode, I always chose to go to the supermarket after nine at night, when the crowd was thinnest, just in case anything untoward happened again. Whenever Aaron was with me, I would always stick to one or two supermarkets, of which I remembered the exact routes we took on the first visit. Woe betide me if I should forget and use a different route, for Aaron had already mapped out the route in his photographic mind the very first time!

Our shopping expeditions always concluded with a fifteen-minute detour up the escalator to the next level, where Aaron would stop by several of his favourite shops to gaze at the exit signs – for about half a minute each. No matter how short of time I might be, I always had to accommodate Aaron and let him complete his ritual. Knowing what I would be in for if I didn't, I would do anything to prevent another outburst from him.

Presently, at age eleven, Aaron's fad for traffic signs has further developed to include directions and road maps. With the maps firmly imprinted in his mind, he can be my eyes and my GPS on the road. I can rely on him whenever I am lost, for he can accurately direct me back to the desired destination. Thankfully, the negative part of his passion with traffic signs is buried and forgotten, now replaced by new and positive ones. While the old had caused me so much pain and distress, the new has saved me from many a distressful moment on the road.

A Traumatic Experience (related to traffic signs)

Aaron at four

Being autistic, Aaron was militant and unrelenting in sticking to rules and regulations, particularly traffic rules. The slightest deviation to any rule was unacceptable to him. A little incident that took place when he was four revealed the extent of his perfectionist obsessive syndrome.

I was driving him to school that fateful morning. There was a nasty traffic jam on the road, and it was getting late. Knowing what it meant for Aaron to arrive late in school and to break his normal routine, I was anxious to get him there on time. Given his predictable pattern of behaviour, it would very likely trigger off a massive tantrum, meaning highly tense emotions and anxiety blown out of proportion. And once the tantrum started, it would be unnerving and could last for hours.

In my eagerness to avoid an impending disaster, I shot past a yellow traffic light. That split second decision was the gravest mistake I made that day. In trying to avert a storm, I hit a tornado instead! Obeying traffic rules was his most sacred obsession, and breaking it was a disaster. It was not just forbidden, but to Aaron it was unforgiveable. Just imagine what ensued after that.

I should have known that nothing escaped his vigilant eyes on the road. But it was too late. Aaron screamed and kicked in rage as if the whole world had collapsed. His fury was escalating by the minute. Everything had gone wrong for him. He demanded a do-over, or 'rewind', as he used to call it. It meant restarting the whole day's programmed routine. This would incorporate waking up from his sleep, brushing his teeth, changing, taking his breakfast, putting his shoes on, and then going back into the car to start the journey all over again to school. Without this replay, he would possibly experience a mental block and would not be able to function. Much as I understood his state of mind, it was virtually impossible to give in to his demand, especially in that heavy traffic.

The deafening din of his screams almost literally drove me out of my wits and sanity. As if that weren't enough, he mustered enough strength in his fury to almost get out of his car seat and grab at the wheel. He behaved like a little out-of-control monster. I tried hard to calm him down but wasn't successful. I thought of stopping the car by the roadside, but that was not possible in the heavy traffic. My heart was pounding frantically, and I could only cry out desperately in my heart that an untoward accident would not happen because of my tussle with him. It was indeed a relief when I finally arrived safely in front of the school gate after such a nerve-racking experience. The one hour on the road felt like ages.

While the danger on the road was over, the stressful episode was far from over. Aaron kicked and screamed in front of the school. As he was much too far into his meltdown and beyond the stage of reasoning and coercion, he could not cooperate with the therapists who came out to help. He refused to be pacified and continued screaming and kicking uncontrollably for hours in front of the school. He did not step into the school and thus missed his therapy sessions that morning. All I could do was watch him helplessly as he unleashed his violent anger. I had no choice but to take him home.

Aaron's tantrum did not subside even on our journey home. It was only after we had reached home that he finally calmed down. By then, I was completely drained and feeling totally defeated and distraught that the whole day had been ruined.

Thank God there was never a repeat of drama quite like that on the road or we both might not have survived the second round!

Aaron at nine

'Dad, aren't you going straight and taking the roundabout?' asked Aaron as we were returning to our apartment. Aaron was about nine and a half years old then. We were on a vacation in New Zealand and staying in a holiday resort in Rotorua.

'No, Aaron,' replied his dad, 'we're taking a shortcut.'

'Oh!' Aaron exclaimed with a tinge of disappointment. Then, with his eyes closed, he added, 'I'm not looking!' just as his dad drove the car anticlockwise around the roundabout and entered the short one-way stretch of the road in the wrong direction. It was not because he feared or was expecting a possible collision with an oncoming car. There was no traffic then. It was because he chose to be oblivious to a traffic violation that was being committed. He only opened his eyes when the car stopped in front of the apartment.

Aaron's reaction might be dismissed as trite, a little childish, or strange. But to me, it was a wonderful coping mechanism for an obsession that had consumed his whole being and controlled his thoughts – and which had often led him to irrational behaviour. It speaks of a milestone of progress which God has wrought in his life. Recalling what he was like before evokes in me a deep sense of gratitude to God.

On the Highway

While travelling on the highway, it was a pleasurable indulgence for Aaron to feast his eyes on the traffic signs, signboards (indicating the distances to various places), and even the inconspicuous, obscure milestones by the roadside. Fatigue and boredom were never a problem for him on a humdrum long journey; in fact, he was strangely stimulated and absorbed by just looking out for the signs and gazing at them meticulously. His mind seemed to keep check, compute, and register every detail of what he had seen, and no discrepancy of any form could escape his eye. On one of our long-distance travels in Malaysia, he alarmingly pointed out that the signboard indicating the distance of 150 kilometres to reach our destination was an error, as we had passed by a signboard earlier that indicated it was 100 kilometres. None of us had noticed it, nor did we pay much attention to it. To Aaron, however, it was an alarming discovery, and he wondered how anyone could have missed something so glaringly unbelievable.

Aaron had such unbridled enthusiasm over traffic signs that he was over the moon with excitement whenever he saw something unusual about them. The difference could be minor, such as the shade of colour, the size, or the arrows shown. When he suddenly noticed an anomaly on a traffic sign one time, he didn't want anyone, especially his sister, to miss such a fascinating sight. 'Alysha, look! Look at the arrow of the sign. Look, it's pointing in the opposite direction! Oh, Alysha, quick or you're going to miss it!' he exclaimed excitedly as he kept nudging his sister to wake up from her snooze.

Alysha was completely nonchalant, and her response was rather dampening and discouraging to Aaron: 'But I'm not interested in traffic signs,' she grumbled, irritated at being disturbed. Aaron could not understand why no one, not even his sister, shared his interest. Then suddenly, the truth hit him: he could be different from everyone else. Turning to me for reassurance, he asked, 'But, Mum, isn't it exciting?' Not wanting to hurt his sensitivities, I agreed that it was.

One day after our holiday in Malaysia, his grandmother asked him casually, 'Aaron, what's the greatest difference to you between Australia and Malaysia?' He was silent for a while, and she asked further if it was the weather, the people, or the buildings. To her great surprise, Aaron blurted an answer she least expected.

'It's the traffic signs.' His grandmother, simulating great interest in the subject, encouraged him to tell her more about it. It was Aaron's turn to be surprised. 'Do you really want to know about it?' he asked.

'Of course,' she replied.

His countenance lifted up with delight to know that someone else shared his interest. Taking a pencil and a few blank sheets of paper, he excitedly started to explain the differences with detailed drawings.

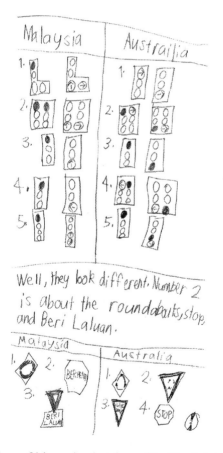

One of his early sketches of traffic lights
and signs, showing the differences

He would gladly go through the litany of explaining anything about traffic signs to anyone who cared to listen. It was a rare treat to him. He was particularly fascinated with the toll plaza in Malaysia, as the like of it was not found in Australia. While it was more a booth in Australia, the plaza toll in Malaysia, with its green roof, sitting in the middle of a highway, looked like a house to him.

It's amazing how the minute details of the signs were clearly and firmly etched in his memory.

(b) Exit signs

The heavens declare the glory of God;
the skies proclaim the works of his hands.
—Psalm 19:1 NIV

We marvel at the perfection and splendour of God's handiwork and the enthralling beauty of His creation. To pause and gaze in admiration at the ethereal hues of the rising sun is our natural response to things that are aesthetically attractive, but to stop and be captivated by something as drab and commonplace as exit signs is quite another thing. Aaron's penchant for traffic signs is only half the story; exit signs are the other 'twin' in his penchant for signage. Exit signs always have a peculiar lure and appeal to him.

During our vacation in Malaysia, we were travelling back to Kuala Lumpur from Johor Bahru one day. We stopped for lunch at the Shahala Coffee Mart at Pagoh. I noticed that Aaron's eyes were fixed on the *keluar* sign there for a slightly longer time than usual. 'Aaron, is this sign any different from all the other *keluar* signs you have seen?' I asked, not expecting an answer. No one had ever shared an interest in the exit sign, and he was excited to explain the differences to me. Like a keen expert on the subject, he offered a detailed explanation.

'Mum, do you notice that the *keluar* sign here has the letters *k-e-l-u-a-r* in green and the background in white?' said Aaron, pointing to the sign.

'Yes,' I answered, 'but don't they all look the same?'

'Of course not,' he said impatiently.

I realized for the first time that most *keluar* signs had the letters in white against a green background. I believed most people were as disinterested and unobservant as I was, for who cares about exit signs, anyway? Aaron, on the other hand, was amazed how anyone could have missed something as obvious as that. I thought that particular sign (green letters against a white background) was the only one of its kind in Malaysia, but Aaron had already listed in his mind the places where the rest of these signs were.

'You can find it in all the *keluar* signs at the Curve shopping complex, at IKEA, and the shops at IKANO,' he explained. 'In the 1-Utama shopping complex, you'll see it only on the ground level and the second level.'

No exit signs in the shopping complexes escaped the detailed scrutiny of his eyes. He elaborated that the one which was the most exciting to him, which I did not even notice, was the one showing a headless figure of a man running. The thrill of seeing that one at a shopping complex was like finding a needle in a haystack.

'Why do you ask so much about the *keluar* sign, Mum?' he asked, clearly surprised but pleased that I was sharing his interest.

'Well, Aaron, is it a good idea that I write a book about you someday and include the *keluar* signs in your book?' I asked.

'But why do you want to write a book about me?' he asked curiously.

Knowing how sensitive he was about being 'special', I explained that God had wonderfully changed him and that he was so different compared to the time when he had many behavioural problems. I also explained that his story would encourage others to be better like him. Thinking that he had overcome autism, he even suggested that the book be titled *All about Aaron: Aaron with Autism and without Autism.*

It was not a problem for Aaron to be distracted by the exit signs when he was on vacation, but it was certainly disconcerting when he went on a school function, such as the school trip to the aquarium. My greatest concern was that he might get distracted gazing at the exit signs and become separated from the rest of the group.

My fears were not unfounded. Two years earlier, when he was five, my husband and I took him to the aquarium for the first time. Much to our disappointment, he showed complete apathy to the aquatic world. While other children would linger and stare with mouths agape at the novelty and the variety of sea creatures in the aquarium, Aaron walked through the aisles with eyes only for the exit signs. For other children, the most exciting part of the aquarium was walking through the water tunnel and watching the fish swimming all around them. But Aaron was different. He refused to go into the tunnel, in spite of our attempts to persuade him, simply because there was no exit sign at the entrance there. Hence, for Aaron's sake, we missed the highlight of the aquarium. A few hours would not be enough for most children at the aquarium, but for Aaron half an hour was already too long. He had exhausted the exit signs within that time and couldn't wait to leave. He became so agitated and impatient that we had to leave shortly after that.

It was as good as not having gone there at all. The trip to the aquarium was such a fiasco, ruined by Aaron's disinterest and lackadaisical attitude towards the richness of colour and life of the aquatic world. I felt foolish having wasted our time and money there that day.

Recalling what happened on the first trip, I had to remind him on the day of this school excursion that the exit sign was off limits for him or he would get left behind by his classmates. I gave him specific instructions that he was to focus on the fish in the aquarium and that when he passed through the doors he was to look straight and not look up nor look back at the exit sign. Knowing that none of his friends shared the same obsession with him, he promised to remind himself to keep his eyes off the exit signs. But he was still anxious and apprehensive about it.

'What if I see the exit sign in the reflection of a glass or mirror and I get distracted?' he asked, realizing how easily he could succumb to the irresistible temptation of the sign, should it appear before him even in a reflection. I assured him that it was not likely to happen and he should not be overly anxious about it. Being very rule abiding, a promise made by him was a promise kept. He succeeded in keeping strictly to my instructions and did not get into any trouble. It was a feat that he was proud of – that he managed not to steal or cast a glance at the exit sign in the aquarium that day.

Since that day, Aaron has overcome the urge to always stop before an exit sign as if to pay homage to it. He can keep his eyes off one, but given the choice, he will still want to feast his eyes on the object of his passion. It is indeed very different from the time when we had to walk out of a restaurant because it did not have an exit sign at the door!

CHAPTER 7

SOCIAL INTERACTIONS AND SKILLS

(a) Non-verbal stage (before four years old)

After a few months of therapy and schooling, Aaron began to speak some words, but not coherent sentences. Unless we showed him either pictures or words, he found it hard to understand when we talked to him. In fact, he learnt to communicate better through pictures and words. I had to set up a display board with pictures and words to help him. Soon the entire display board was filled with pictures and words that he could respond to. He was indeed extremely visual.

Aaron also learnt how not to always use the 'red' (shouting) voice but to use the 'yellow' (soft-pitched) voice and 'orange' (normal-pitched) voice. He often had to be reminded to use the 'yellow' voice when he wanted something. Though it was gradual, we could see his progress in shouting less and using more words.

However, as Aaron could not understand any verbal language, I was not able to make him understand that I could not be with him all the time and that it was all right for my parents to look after him.

One night my husband and I had to attend a fund-raising dinner in Aaron's special school, and my parents were going to look after Aaron and his sister, Alysha. I had no choice but to slip off quietly with my husband when Aaron was engrossed in playing with his traffic signs and watching his favourite video programs on the television.

It was only a short while after we left that he started looking for me. He flew into an uncontrollable rage when he realized that I was not at home with him. He ran down the stairs screaming for me and wanted to open the front door forcibly to get out. The screams got louder and louder, and my parents could do nothing to pacify him. He refused to come upstairs but continued screaming and occasionally banging on the door.

My mother desperately showed him a note saying that his mum had gone out for dinner. She tried to explain to him that his mum would be back soon. But that did not calm him down. He was also hungry and thirsty, with a full bladder, but he refused his milk, his favourite cookies, or anything my mother offered him. The more she tried to pacify him, the more he cried. It was best to leave him alone. Going near him with pictures and words showing 'milk', 'bread', and 'toilet' only infuriated him further. He was used to only me, his carer, feeding him or helping him go to the toilet.

My parents didn't know what to do; they felt helpless. If Aaron couldn't hold his bladder and were to wet himself, that would lead to a greater hullaballoo. What a relief for my parents when he finally relented and screamed 'Toilet!' He allowed my dad to rush him to the toilet. But he still did not give up waiting at the stairs. He cried incessantly until he was tired out. Exhausted, his screams finally subsided to a soft moaning until he fell asleep. My husband and I returned home at eleven that evening and heard about Aaron's tantrum. We were relieved that our tension for the night was over. It was tough, but I believed it was good training for Aaron to get used to my being away from him at times, other than the times he was at school (he had got used to the routine of going to school.)

We later found out that it helped to prepare him mentally beforehand that I would be out for dinner and my mother was to be the one to give him his milk and supper, while my father was to take him to the toilet. He resisted the first few times, but gradually he began to accept small changes in his usual routines.

However, I still needed to be around him most of the time. It was my job to put him to sleep, and he was not willing for anyone else to take over that role. It was quite some time before my husband and I could go out occasionally while my parents looked after him and his sister at home.

(b) Antisocial behaviour

'Hi, Aaron,' Aaron's dad said affectionately after coming home from work one evening.

'Hi, Dad,' Aaron responded.

'How was school today, Aaron?'

'Good,' Aaron replied matter-of-factly. This standard much-rehearsed and predictable answer didn't mean much in essence.

'What did you do in school today?' his dad probed. Silence. The question was too general and too unstructured for his mind to process a spontaneous response. Having to sieve through the mass of trivial, detailed, unrelated information to arrive at a condensed, simplified summary of salient facts was a task too challenging and mind-boggling for his natural cognitive ability. In other words, he couldn't see the wood for the trees.

His dad, understanding this handicap in his autistic spectrum, decided to break the question into manageable small parts that were context-and-content specific. 'Did you have sports today?' asked his dad.

'Yes, we had rugby,' he answered without any hesitation.

'What position did you play?' asked his dad.

'Full back,' he responded.

If his dad had asked Aaron to describe the dynamics of how the game was played, the question would have been equally daunting for Aaron. His best attempt in answering it would probably lack coherence and clarity. He might fare better in just explaining a few rules of the game.

Though a conversation with Aaron (age ten) was unanimated and even stilted, he had already come a long way from being totally uncommunicative and even antisocial. Still, he was often lost in his own world, oblivious to his surroundings and the people talking to him. When he was younger, he used to build a wall around himself and enjoyed 'hugging the shadows'. It was as if his inner world overwhelmed him so completely that he was shut off from the outside world. His world revolved around himself and perhaps only me, as his main carer, the only one in his inner circle. I was his security blanket and his Rock of Gibraltar in his times of anxiety and need. His dad, sister, and grandparents were in the outer circle of his hierarchical spheres of attachment. Everyone else was irrelevant.

Before he turned six, he was completely antisocial. Any visitor to the home was unwelcome and even disturbing to him. He made no qualms about displaying his blatant hostility and standoffish manners towards the visitor. He was incorrigible and unteachable in any form of social manners or etiquette.

He would be extremely difficult when the visitor tried to carry on a conversation with me. To him it was a big no-no.

He was not going to tolerate it, for in his mind, he had the sole monopoly of my attention and no one should rob or usurp him of that privilege. He would cup my mouth with his hand to prevent me from talking to anyone. The moment he heard my voice, he would scream so that I could not conduct any conversation. He would react in exasperation by griping, fuming, and fretting. The visitor would usually take the hint and, feeling very uncomfortable, would take his or her leave earlier than intended. That seemed to be his moment of triumph.

His demeanour would immediately change, and he would be at his best behaviour. He would turn civil, bid farewell, and even usher the visitor to the door. His smug smile seemed to suggest that he prided himself on being successful in his quest. Compared to a normal child, his behaviour would be regarded as outright impudence, wilfulness, and defiance. However, having learnt about autism and understanding Aaron as an autistic child, I could see his behaviour from a different perspective. He saw the visitor's presence as an invasion of space, and that evoked great anxiety and unrest in him. His space included only his family members, and anyone else was an intruder.

At home, Aaron's little sister, Alysha, who was two years younger than he was, had to pay a heavy price for her natural sisterly affection towards her brother. She suffered for wanting to draw close to him. Without naturally developed emotions as an autistic child, he could not respond with love. His sister was at his mercy, especially when she crawled near him. His instant reflex action was to push or hit her, but little Alysha was too young to understand rejection and his negative vibes. It didn't deter her in the least from drawing near to him. In fact, her mere endearing cry 'ko ko' ('older brother') each time she saw him was enough to incite him to attack her. He could not understand her overtures of affection, which were simply an irritation and nuisance to him. I had to keep an eye on both of them constantly and keep them as far apart as possible too. Alysha always had to be protected from his aggression.

Outside home, his outrageous, antisocial behaviour and mannerisms were alarmingly distressful. He snarled and grunted in disgust at anyone who showed a friendly gesture towards him. How I wish I could tell the whole world just to ignore him. Who would have thought that an innocuous greeting like 'Hi, Aaron!' could set him off? To say that I often cringed in embarrassment over his rather bizarre behaviour is a gross understatement. The truth was, his behaviour rubbed off on me, and I was beginning to withdraw from people and become an unfriendly recluse. My personality underwent a drastic transformation. I became morose and dispirited. I lost interest in people, mostly in interacting with them. It was a very lonely path. The only people I thought who could truly understand my plight were my support group and the mothers of Aaron's friends in the special school. I turned down more and more invitations to social functions, much to the dismay of my husband, who simply enjoyed socials. So ashamed was I of Aaron's temper tantrums and his aberrant social behaviour that I shied away from people, even during those social gatherings that I could not avoid attending. I always found myself in a safe corner with Aaron, away from the madding crowd. I tried escaping from being noticed and was happiest when no one came to show concern or draw me back to the party.

Of those functions that I was prepared to attend, there were a few where I didn't even get past the door. When our Iranian neighbour invited us to his house-warming party, Aaron started screaming at the doorstep at the sight of everyone wearing shoes in the house. It was something he was not accustomed to (outdoor shoes are not worn inside Chinese homes), and it was therefore unacceptable to him. While my husband stayed on at the party, I found a good excuse to leave immediately with Aaron.

On another occasion, we were going to a friend's birthday party. As we approached the house, Aaron saw that the house had no postbox with the number of the house on it. He became so alarmed that he refused to enter the house. We had no choice but to go straight home, unable to attend the party.

One day when Aaron's dad brought him home, he could not drive straight into the garage because there was a car blocking the entrance. My friend had come to get some Entertainment Books to help me in my fund-raising project. We were engaged in a short conversation and did not realize that Aaron and his dad were coming home at that time. Aaron clearly didn't expect to be unable to get into the garage immediately, and he was unduly perturbed by it. His dad made a round in his car to give my friend time to leave. Unfortunately, by the time they were back, my friend had still not left. This was the last straw that broke Aaron's cool; his tantrum was sparked off and lasted for more than half an hour.

Going to church each Sunday was no longer a joy but a chore and something to dread. While the service was under way, I would be in the playroom with Aaron. The only rare occasions I could enjoy relative peace were the times when no other children and mothers were in the playroom.

Even at four years old, Aaron's play was very insular. He had not learned to share. If he wanted a particular toy, he must have it, even if it meant snatching it from another child. If the other child was not complaining and the mother was accommodating, I even chose to condone Aaron's inconsiderate and selfish behaviour for the sake of peace. I had hardly any choice, for I was not prepared to face the inevitable tumultuous outcome of his tantrum. But most of the time, the vociferous demands and fights of the kids over the toys created a big hue and cry, and Aaron was always in the centre of the chaos. Those who had observed Aaron's unruly and appalling behaviour might consider him a tragic victim of parental ineptitude – and me a pathetic failure as a mother. The way they winced conveyed the suggestion that I ought to be attending a parenting course on disciplining children. Putting myself in their shoes, without having any knowledge of autism, I might have been as judgmental.

On one occasion, I left the room for a short while to get a drink while Aaron was absorbed in playing with something in the playroom. When I came back shortly after that, I found him crying uncontrollably. A member of the church apparently took it upon himself to discipline Aaron. He had told Aaron not to take something out of a little girl's bag. After three times of 'I warn you!' he hit Aaron on the hand. He did not understand that Aaron, being autistic, could not understand him. Aaron had no language yet, though he was four, and he could not understand any instructions, let alone the sentence 'I warn you!'

If I had wanted to stop Aaron, I would only use the word no and take him away from the scene. Even this would stir up a small commotion, so the thought of a total stranger hitting him for a supposed wrongdoing which he had no understanding of was outrageous.

There was hardly a week in church when I could enjoy the worship without being bogged down by stress. No one, not even his dad, could give me a break in seeing to Aaron. Aaron needed only me, his carer, and no one else. Because of his constant stressful demands on me, I was worn out mentally, emotionally, and spiritually. I felt defeated within and without. With hardly any spiritual input, my spiritual life reached an all-time low. However, despite being reduced to a state of quiet resignation and desperation, I pressed on in the spirit and attended church regularly, even though my flesh was weak.

If my Sundays in church were far from being worshipful and stress-free, my weekdays were far worse. An incident that happened just outside my house almost burst the camel's back. That evening, as usual, after coming back from Aaron's school, I drove my car into the garage of the town house. I left Alysha in the car and then took Aaron to the front to enter the house through the main door. That was Aaron's ritual. He had to ring the bell and enter through the proper door, not through the garage.

A neighbour happened to pass by at that precise moment, before Aaron could ring the bell. She greeted us with a friendly hi, a greeting that became an unexpected catalyst that ignited a series of high-tension dramas. The greeting had no part in Aaron's ritual or routine which he followed regimentally, so he reeled in fury and shrieked at the top of his voice, leaving the neighbour nonplussed, wondering what offense she had committed. Before long, he was not only crying and screaming but also pushing, kicking, and rolling on the ground. It was one of his worst tantrums ever. My efforts to calm him were futile, and it went on for almost an hour.

Meanwhile, poor Alysha, who was left alone in the car, was crying in hunger and fear. I had no choice but to leave Aaron outside the house by himself while I went into the garage, picked up Alysha, and took her into the house and upstairs.

Aaron became almost hysterical in his rage and was dripping wet with tears. I was unable to get him to enter the house. Finally, when he was almost hoarse from crying and screaming, I heard him shouting something about 'pissing in the park'. His bladder was almost bursting, yet he was too obstinate to come into the house to use the toilet. I had no choice but to send an SOS to my in-laws, as his dad was at work. They arrived half an hour later to take him to the park, where he eased himself by a particular tree, as he had done before. By God's grace, Aaron had calmed down by the time he returned home with his grandparents.

It's a wonder I didn't break down or fold under pressure, trying to cope with the cramping restrictions of a meaningless struggle. The earnest prayers and intercession of my family and well-meaning Christian friends must have been surrounding me. Most of all, it must have been the hand of God sustaining me through it all, for He is indeed 'able to do immeasurably more than all we ask or imagine, according to His power that is at work within us' (Eph. 3:20 NIV). As He promised, He had not tested me beyond the point that I could take (1 Cor. 10:13).

(c) Insular and repetitive play

'Children, stop playing! Time for lunch!' I shouted at the top of my voice for the third time. My voice was drowned in the pandemonium of the children's romping and stomping, frolicking, and shouting in their play. Alysha and the girls put their Barbie dolls aside and came to the table, whilst Aaron and the boys were too enthralled in their rough and boisterous game to have even heard my call. Eventually, they came – panting and heaving and smelling of sweat – when I managed to round them up physically.

Watching Aaron playing with the boys, one would not have thought that social playing was a skill that did not come naturally for Aaron. He had to learn it through years of play therapy. Had it not been for the therapy, his play would still be insular and repetitive in nature; no normal child would want to play with him. He would not have learnt to take turns and be tolerant with others. In fact, until he was about six, he used to demand that others play by his rules. He once became so frustrated when the other children ignored him as he tried to impose his rules on them that he shouted in despair, 'Why is no one listening to me?'

His sister consoled him and said, 'It's all right, Aaron. They're just normal kids.'

Alysha always looking out for Aaron

Before he learnt this skill, there were a number of angst-ridden and embarrassing incidents associated with his self-centred and insular play. I can never forget the day when my already scarred and shattered self-image as a mother took a further beating from the nasty remarks I received because of his behaviour.

We were at a shopping centre where, at one section of the children's play area, there was Thomas the Tank Engine, complete with the main station, substations, railway tracks, and the different trains. Thomas the Tank Engine was one of Aaron's favourite toys, and he could be absorbed playing with the entire train set for an hour or more. He had to go through the motion of every train chugging out from the main station and completing the whole journey on the railway track. Unfortunately, he could not monopolize the toy, as it was in a public place. In the midst of it, young children and toddlers would come and interrupt his play by putting their trains on the track. To Aaron, they were not just intruding in his play; they were also not playing by his rules. His single-mindedness told him that the trains should not suddenly appear in the middle of the track. They must start out from the main train station. What the little ones did was intolerable to Aaron, and he would inadvertently make them cry by either pushing them away or throwing their trains off the track. Their mothers, grabbing the children away, would stare at me in disbelief. The expressions on their faces spoke volumes: in condoning Aaron's act, I was part of the equation to my son's belligerence and detestable behaviour.

An older boy about Aaron's age came along one day, and he waited patiently for his turn to play since Aaron was not willing to share with him. After waiting about fifteen minutes, he started fidgeting and complaining to his mother, who hinted to me that it was about time Aaron stopped playing so that her son could have his turn. Feeling hopeless about offering an explanation to the woman that Aaron's obsessive-compulsive trait would not allow him to stop halfway through his game, I tried getting Aaron to leave, knowing that he would not budge until he had finished his game. My seemingly half-hearted attempts must have given her the impression that I was blithely unperturbed and unconcerned about her son's feelings in not getting his rightful turn. Half an hour later, she left in a huff, with her boy crying, but not without first giving me an earful of what she thought of Aaron – and me, as an incompetent, unfit mother. The barbed language she used left me not reeling in anger but rather feeling defeated and distraught.

Once bitten, twice shy, as the saying goes. I lost confidence in venturing into that shopping centre again, for the unpleasant, painful memories have lingered on until the present day.

At home, it was a rare treat if Aaron could play with his toys peacefully and quietly. His strange fixation about things being in a particular order or spot and his resistance to change were projected onto his toys. A missing part in his toys or a missing letter or number would be enough to ignite his crazed anger and loud screams. It would throw me into total disarray, searching frantically for the elusive parts until I found them. As such, I would painstakingly ensure that at the end of each day, every one of his toys was in proper order and place and nothing was amiss.

A musical toy he had was the most troublesome. This toy would play a musical tune, and the picture (that of a bridge) would move at the same time when it was turned on.

The troublesome toy

When the music stopped, he would expect the picture to stop with the bridge precisely at the central position. It seldom happened. If it stopped in a position away from the centre, even if it was less than a centimetre away, he would scream in utter frustration. By trial and error, I quickly had to try to get the picture back to the exact spot that he demanded. There was no way I could make Aaron understand that perfect synchrony was more of a coincidence than a norm and that missing the mark was to be expected. I resorted to hiding this troublesome toy, and others like it, in a safe place away from him, his sister, or any other child. What a pity that such wonderful wholesome toys for children had to be kept in cold storage. These toys were safely 'buried' and didn't see light until a few years later, when Aaron was six and had gotten over that difficult phase.

(d) Retreating into his own inner world

Had Aaron not been autistic, I would have chided him many a time over his carelessness and inattentiveness when listening to the instructions of his teachers, coaches, or instructors. He often conveyed to me only incomplete or inaccurate messages that resulted in dire consequences. And then the blame would always be on me when he did not bring to school his homework, his correct attire for the occasion, the paraphernalia needed for his project, and a host of other things. Irrational and unreasonable as it was, he actually expected me to have prior knowledge of what was needed for his school's activities, irrespective of what he had told me the night before. Even if his teacher could excuse him for any mistake made, he could not excuse himself or me, his carer. Once it was made, his anxiety would be precipitated. Oftentimes the degree of his anxiety was not in direct proportion to the seriousness of it. Even a trivial slip in the most extenuating circumstances would be critical for him if he stood shamefully alone in his ordeal. Having a partner in crime helped alleviate the severity of his anxiety. If there were other friends in the same predicament, it did not matter in the least, even if the punishment was harsh. Getting a rebuke and going for the detention class was not a big deal to him; it was acceptable, as it was part of the equation of a rule broken.

One day the children were going by bus on an excursion that the school had organized. He got on the bus and discovered that his other friends had their school jackets on; he had not brought his. He panicked. His teachers spotted him seated quietly by himself on the bus, tears streaming down his eyes. He did not want to be the only one who stood out as different, without his jacket. A teacher tried to comfort and assure him that the jacket was not compulsory, as he was already in his school uniform. But he could not be pacified. Fortunately, a little while later, one other student boarded the bus without a jacket. He immediately stopped crying. That saved the day and the outing from being a total disaster for him.

Knowing how prone Aaron was to missing out instructions, I had to solicit the help of his class teacher in writing out important instructions in his book for me to follow up. I also had to countercheck constantly with a friend whose son was in the same class with Aaron, just to make sure that nothing was amiss, especially during special occasions, like the speech day, sports day, or a school excursion.

Being autistic and having a visual mind, Aaron had limitations in processing and following instructions, especially if they were long, unstructured, and unrelated, more so if the instructions were too general (like a public announcement) and not specifically directed to him. The rapid rate with which the instructions were spoken would often exceed his brain's processing speed, and he would get in a fuddle. It was as if his nerve centre had experienced an information overload which caused it to go berserk and automatically shut down. To cope with the confusion, he distracted himself and replaced his thoughts with his favourite ones (perhaps the traffic signs or other things that interested him within his view), hence causing him to drift off naturally into his dreamland. Being blurry or dreamy is still his innate inborn propensity.

His dreaminess and slowness in perceiving instructions also made him a ready victim in some outdoor games. Right from Year One at school, he used to ask me, 'Mum, why do I always have to be the 'baddie' in the game?' I had no answer to his question, although I understood why. It's because he was slow in understanding the rules of the game, especially when it was played for the first time, and he lagged behind the others. Besides, he was also not as quick-footed or agile in his motor skills. Thus he would end up being the last person to run when the cue was given, so he was therefore the 'baddie' each time. Even when he was older, he still confronted me with a similar question, except for a slight difference in the terminology: 'Mum, why must I always be the 'it' in the game?' Whatever the outdoor game was, he was a victim of his natural handicap.

Mulling pessimistically on Aaron's setbacks, I used to wonder if his fragile self-esteem could stand the constant onslaught of heartless ridicule, bullying, and injustice in his adult life. With a sense of foreboding, I could imagine the countless problems that he could encounter if he were to miss out on important data, especially in momentous situations. But God assured me that I should not worry ahead of time, though I might have to accept that he would still be dreamy occasionally and drift into his own world. I just had to trust God to be there for Aaron at all times and to protect his self-esteem from being frayed by the apathy and carelessness of those who might misunderstand him.

In a recent athletics carnival in Aaron's school, God provided a way out of his predicament: sending a good friend named Christopher to be his guardian angel. Christopher's brother was also autistic, so he was well trained and experienced in seeing to and watching out for his brother's dreamy tendencies. At the carnival, Christopher reminded and alerted Aaron when it was almost Aaron's turn to run. When he told Aaron to get ready, Aaron realized that he had not brought the proper attire for the carnival, with the colour that represented his team. He panicked and felt helpless. He could not think of how to solve his problem. Christopher was quick to act. Rising to the occasion, he borrowed an attire from one of the boys in the same team, a child who had completed his turn. He gave it to Aaron and wasted no time in helping Aaron quickly change. Thanks to Christopher, Aaron was ready to run when his turn came.

Even today, at age eleven, Aaron still gets 'lost' in a crowd or an environment where there is a diverse hotchpotch of noise or information. His natural defence mechanism is to switch off and to find refuge in the sanctuary of his own world. In a setting where people are engaged in social chit-chat, he normally stays out of it for the simple reason that he cannot filter and assimilate what is relevant. Unless the conversation is directed at him specifically, he normally remains antisocial and uninvolved. Though he may be physically there with the others, his thoughts are elsewhere. He gets lost in a crowd that is immersed in the sea of unstructured talk and confusing voices.

(e) First speech therapy session

This was a most difficult decision for me. Faced with Aaron's poor verbal skills at the age of five, I desperately sought a good speech therapist for him. I knew he needed extra special coaching on top of what he was already getting at his special school.

When I finally found a reputable speech therapist for him, the thought of driving all the way there and back (seventy kilometres) for an hour's session each week was enough to put me off. There was also the nagging fear that the sacrifice might be all for nothing. Besides the distance, I had to consider the high cost involved. I also asked myself if I could cope with one more agenda added to my overstretched schedule. I was already exhausted from seeing to all of Aaron's programmes and activities in addition to all my other responsibilities at home. I was prepared to go to any extent and any sacrifice for Aaron's sake, but I also had to contend with the issue of Aaron's hostile reception to any stranger. His new therapist, a total stranger, would pose a threat to him, and he might not be a willing participant in cooperating with her. However, despite my scepticism and negative thoughts, I decided to give it a shot. Perhaps I feared being plagued by guilt for depriving Aaron of what might help him. I also had God's encouragement from His word that 'our sufficiency is from God' (2 Cor. 3:5).

I will never forget the nightmare that marked Aaron's first day with the therapist. On arrival at the therapist's house, I rang the doorbell and the therapist came out to greet Aaron by saying hello. But Aaron was overtly hostile and ignored her greeting altogether. The therapist wasn't prepared to accept this cold reception and was determined to get him out of it. She repeated the greeting for a second and third time, but it elicited absolutely no response from Aaron each time. I thought to myself that the therapist, in understanding Aaron's antisocial behaviour, should have excused Aaron, for it was his first time meeting her. But the therapist doggedly insisted that Aaron should respond politely before he could be allowed into the house. She felt that Aaron had to learn good social etiquette. So it became a match of patience and resistance on both ends;

Aaron was as obstinate about not giving in to her as she was determined to get him to do so.

A full fifteen minutes passed, after which the therapist instructed me to go into the house and to leave Aaron alone at the door to suffer the consequence of his obstinacy. As expected, Aaron broke into his frenzied rage when he saw me leaving his side. It was like hell breaking loose. My heart went out to him. It pained me to see Aaron's harsh punishment, but I had no choice but to cooperate with the therapist. While he was screaming hysterically, his eyes were following me appealingly to the door as if to beg me to rescue him from his straits. I had to appear strong and to ignore him heartlessly as I closed the door behind me. My heart was pounding as I heard him screaming his heart out pathetically outside the door. Minutes ticked by, and it stretched to a full half hour. Still, both the therapist and Aaron refused to relent. In my heart at that time, I really felt let down and disillusioned. I wished the therapist had not been so harsh with Aaron. It was also such a waste of precious time which could have been used profitably for his therapy. Imagine having to pay exorbitantly just to watch Aaron being disciplined – and for such a trivial offence!

I'd almost reached the end of the tether when Aaron finally blurted out the word 'hello' angrily and reluctantly, as if in protest. But that was not good enough for the therapist. Aaron had to repeat the greeting until it sounded civil and acceptable to her. It was indeed a great relief for me when Aaron finally complied. Thus far, no one had been able to break Aaron's strong will. I marvelled that for once persistence broke resistance!

By the time Aaron was allowed into the house, there was only time for a brief introductory lesson with the therapist. Soon the session was over, so he could play with the toys while the therapist spoke to me. Aaron interrupted the conversation and demanded my immediate attention. In my fear of his outburst and tantrum, I had inadvertently been giving in to his incessant demands before, though I knew it served only to reinforce his unacceptable behaviour. Besides, Aaron had always considered it his sacred right and privilege to have direct immediate access to me, his carer, and nothing and nobody could ever stop him. But this time Aaron could not get away with his insolent behaviour. He was reprimanded for interrupting the conversation and was told to wait patiently for his turn to speak. As expected, he kicked up a big fuss and another tantrum ensued. Fortunately, it lasted for only ten minutes.

No sooner had he gotten over it than the therapist told him to put away the toys. Again he refused to obey, and when he was forced to do so, he screamed again. I could not really blame him, as I had always been the one to pack up his toys at home. By the time Aaron's angst-ridden drama was over, he was exhausted and drenched in sweat. To me, it was a nerve-racking and daunting experience. I wondered if anything good was accomplished that fateful afternoon other than a breaking down of Aaron's strong will.

When the time came for the next session the following week, I feared the worst, as Aaron had expressed his anger and reluctance to meet the therapist again. I anticipated another tumultuous affair, perhaps worse! When we finally arrived at the doorstep of the therapist's house, it was with much trepidation that I pressed the doorbell. Thank God the traumatic episode at the door was not repeated. Aaron somehow had learnt that the therapist's boundary was firm and he was not about to get his way with her. Much to my pleasant surprise, it was a completely different scenario. The therapist had managed to break through Aaron's initial resistance and had helped him to understand boundaries. He complied by greeting her without any fuss.

Though the therapist's sessions had been trying at times, I could see Aaron's gradual progress. With each passing week, Aaron began to take to the therapist better, and by the fourth week, there was hardly any resistance. She could then carry out an enjoyable productive lesson with him.

In retrospect, I am glad I persevered and did not give in to discouragement after the initial ordeal. The greatest victory was that his strong will and insistence on having his own way were gradually eroded to give way to clear boundaries. Subsequently, I was also able to set rules and boundaries for him to follow. Discipline and obedience became a part of his learnt behaviour. Patience and perseverance ultimately paid off in the end.

(f) A strong sense of social justice

Aaron exhibited an extraordinary strong sense of social justice. He was rigidly intolerant of anything that did not conform to his blanket concept of right and wrong. Mistreatment or injustice in any form would be almost insurmountable for him to cope with. In this fallen world, where malicious manipulation and foul play is rife, his naivety and idealistic expectations of fair play would only make him a ready candidate for exploitation and unkind treatment, even in a safe environment. I dread to think how debilitating and devastating it would be for him to suffer injustice of any kind, being misunderstood, maligned, or unjustifiably attacked by those with critical spirits.

An incident happened in his school recently when he was ten. I went to pick Aaron up from school one evening after his athletics practice. His eyes were red and puffed up, obviously from a bout of crying. 'Mum,' he reported as he got into the car, 'I was accused, but I didn't do it.' I stiffened up in alarm. It was unlike Aaron to report about anything that happened in school unless it was drastic. Knowing that he was incapable of telling a lie, I probed to find out what had really happened. Through his incoherent sputtering, I managed to put together the bits of information.

It was during the time when the boys were having their football practice. While walking behind the physical education teacher, the boys got a little playful and rowdy. They were pushing and shoving one another around. When the teacher turned around, he saw Aaron among the boys who misbehaved. He picked on Aaron and rebuked him. Aaron protested vehemently that he wasn't the one involved in the act, but the teacher told him off harshly. The teacher even added some snide remarks about the poor grade that Aaron would receive as a result. This was not what affected him most. He accepted the threat about the poor grade without any problem, for it was what he thought he deserved for his poor motor skills. But what he couldn't take was being accused of something he was innocent of. It violated his sense of social justice. He felt totally crushed in his spirit and broke down in tears. He sobbed uncontrollably by himself even after the lesson was over. Some of his friends rallied around him to console him.

I was resolute in getting to the root of the matter. I discovered from one of Aaron's friends that Aaron was hardly the PE teacher's star student, being weak in his motor skills. The teacher always picked on him and told him off, saying such things as, 'Aaron, what is wrong with you? Can't you kick the ball harder?' He might have had good intentions of wanting Aaron to improve, but it was all through negative reinforcement. Obviously, he had no idea that Aaron was autistic and had already come a long way from the time when he had to do the very basics of muscular coordination. The way Aaron was 'coached' was certainly no help to his already jaded self-esteem.

The incident prompted me to speak to the teachers openly about Aaron's condition. The principal of the school, who had known about Aaron's condition, did not make it public knowledge to his teachers, as he believed strictly in observing the privacy law. I was glad that the main PE teacher in charge (not his assistant, who was hard on Aaron) was understanding, for he had had experience handling autistic children in another school in the UK. He assured me that he would see to it that Aaron be given the right motivation to excel. The matter was brought to a peaceful and happy closure, thanks to God, who turned even unpleasant things around for good.

Another dramatic incident happened when we were holidaying in Singapore. He was eight then. This time the incident involved his sister, but its repercussion was much more on him than on his sister. After alighting from the train (MRT), we were walking in the MRT station when suddenly Alysha felt a sharp pain and a tug of her long hair from behind. Alysha happened to be in the path of a hyperactive child in the quest of doing something outrageously naughty to satisfy his lust for mischief and excitement. It was a hit-and-run case. The little boy ran off and disappeared as quickly as he came. His mother was trailing him, and she apologized profusely for her son's unruly behaviour, but she had to rush off in pursuit of the boy.

Alysha soon got over the shock of the sudden painful tug of her hair and stopped crying after about ten minutes, but Aaron could not get over the injustice of the whole incident. He could not accept the fact that the boy had gotten away scot-free and justice was not meted out on him for his misdeed. He launched into an angry barrage of complaints about the boy and the mother. He said repeatedly, 'If I see the boy again, I will take a stick and hit him … If I see the boy again, I will ask the policemen to catch him and put him in jail … If I see his mother, she must also go to jail ...' As the thoughts of the incident were reverberating in his mind, we had to bear his endless repetitions, which were much like an unstoppable record player. There were only short intermissions in between when something interesting distracted him. You can imagine how relieved we were when he finally went to bed that night. The next day, we were cautious not to tread on subjects that would remind him of the incident, lest the repetition, likened to 'dripping of water', would continue further, perhaps spiced with more colourful and revengeful ideas.

Aaron's sense of social justice is not only about himself and about his need to defend himself against injustice. It is also evident in the way he champions the right of the battered or wronged. The maxim 'Discretion is the better part of valour' will never be fully understood by him. He knows not the art of weighing all things in their right proportion, perspective, and timing. He does not realize that the universe does not always operate neatly according to predictable, reliable and just rules. Rightly or wrongly, he sticks his neck out to speak for the person he believes to be in the right. This may be noble in itself, but in the way he does it, the consequence may not always be so. In his matter of fact, direct, blunt and even offensive way, he is not capable of couching the truth in the most palatable form. Lacking the gift of social grace and interpersonal skills, the truth may be expressed in its most raw and uncouth manner, without the use of euphemism, subtle tact, or implied inoffensive sarcasm.

In one instance, my mum heard Alysha telling her friend that her friend's house was small compared to hers. My mum advised Alysha not to make her friend feel bad by commenting on the smallness of the friend's house. Alysha, feeling embarrassed about it, softly denied having said that. When

Aaron heard her denial, he immediately jumped to her defence and spoke up peevishly for her, saying, 'Alysha didn't say that, Por Por [Grandmother]. You are a liar!' My mum must have been shocked by such an obtrusive, disrespectful accusation, but she knew better than to get furious and to argue with him. She knew that Aaron had no clue about the negative, offensive implication of calling someone a liar. Aaron had used the word literally and indiscriminately. Besides, it was pointless, as it was unlikely that he would relent once his mind was made up. Because he couldn't lie, he least expected anyone else, more so his sister, to have done so.

It is laudable to speak the truth without fear or favour, especially for those in positions of authority, but it is quite another story for Aaron. I can imagine Aaron landing himself into more trouble than he can envisage if he tries to champion the right of someone inappropriately. Calling a spade a spade with no skill in sugar-coating, he may offend without even realizing it.

Stretching my imagination further, the worst scenario is that being so naturally trusting, he may be deceived into believing in the wrong person or the wrong cause without first verifying the facts. Lacking discernment, he is not able to read between the lines nor take cues from a person's body language. His undeterred noble intentions and unflinching combat against social injustice may then backfire and will only end in his suffering the worst horrors of disillusionment, humiliation, defeat, and despair.

I can only pray that when he grows up, he will develop wisdom to exercise his sense of justice in the right context and in ways that do not transcend the boundaries of conventional social norms.

CHAPTER 8

EMOTIONAL INACCESSIBILITY AND EXTREME EMOTIONS

(a) Emotional inaccessibility

The atmosphere was charged with emotions and tinged with sadness. It was the last day of school for the year, and some students were leaving the school. Aaron was leaving the school he had attended for three years to go to a bigger school that was nearer our home. Teachers and students were hugging the school-leavers with bleary eyes and choked emotions. One of the students even burst out in tears. Aaron appeared lost and confused, unprepared for the ethos of love and concern outwardly poured out by his teachers and friends. He was ill at ease and seemed out of place in the setting, not because he was unfeeling and detached but because he felt that the sadness was an incongruent emotion that did not befit the occasion. As a matter of fact and natural progression of events, he and several others were moving on to another school, and he found it strange that the occasion to rejoice should evoke any feelings of sadness. It just did not fit neatly with his sense of logic based on set predictable perimeters. Small wonder his friends' natural emotional response of tears blew his mind.

The students were asked to pray for one another. Most of them prayed for their friends, their teachers, or their school. When it was Aaron's turn to pray, he was brief and to the point. He only prayed that he would not get lost in his new school!

Being autistic, Aaron was born emotionally inaccessible. He lacks the ability to perceive or identify emotions, let alone understand them. A sense of compassion or empathy is not innate in him, nor is he equipped with basic relational skills. He can be emotionally oblivious to the feelings of others in any kind of emotional situation.

Before the age of five, he related to people, objects, and events in abnormal ways. His impaired and delayed speech exacerbated the problem. He was too unusually preoccupied with objects to be aware of people and to connect with them. People, especially strangers, were nonentities and were completely irrelevant to him. It was repugnant for him to be cuddled and touched, especially on the most sensitive part of his body, his head. An affectionate pat on the head could provoke him to react savagely. He made no eye contact when he was spoken to, and he isolated himself in his own world most of the time.

As Aaron was emotionally deficient, he lacked the ability to read facial cues. When he was younger, he could not decipher the expressions of anger or disapproval on a person's face, hence his continued misbehaviour, as if in defiance. This emotional handicap, coupled with the absence of language, explained his overt indifference and unresponsiveness when he was reprimanded. He appeared blatantly impertinent and incorrigible.

Aaron had to be taught how to read emotions from facial expressions. It was like learning the basic ABCs of emotions. His therapists gave him drawings depicting various kinds of facial expressions, such as happiness, sadness, anger, and surprise.

He had to study these diagrams intently and learn to apply them in practice. I became his learning tool. Whenever I showed some emotions on my face, he would immediately stop me midway and ask, 'Are you happy?' or, 'Are you angry?' or, 'Are you sad?' Whenever he couldn't make sense of what someone was saying, he would try to figure out the emotion from the facial expression by trying to match it with the diagrams he had memorized. However, it wasn't a straightforward equation for him to grasp, because facial expressions sometimes move and change too fast. Often thrown into utter confusion and frustration, he would retreat into his own world to cope with it.

He gradually learnt how to relate the diagrams to his own emotion and to apply them in practice. His simulated and contorted facial expressions, which reflected his 'manufactured' versions of the drawings, often appeared artificial, exaggerated, and comical. When asked to smile before a camera, he would put on an animated plastic smile, as close a replica to the drawing as possible.

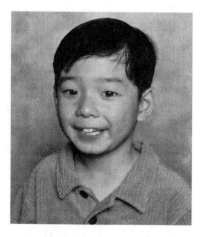

Aaron with his put-on 'plastic' smile

We often could not help sniggering in amusement, but realizing how painstaking an attempt he had made to model the most precise and polished version of the diagram he had learnt, we controlled ourselves. Besides, it would strike his raw nerve and fragile emotions, causing him hurt and discouragement.

Despite his emotional handicap, Aaron had learnt to hug and cuddle by the time he was six years old. Through practice, he has been able to respond appropriately in any emotional or social setting. He is still working on and struggling in the area of empathy. He has also learnt to be considerate and to think of others' needs, but it is more a relational skill that he has mastered rather than a feeling that he has developed naturally through the years. To be able to have an accurate mature perception of emotions will remain a predicament to him. His innate responses are more centred on himself and his needs. By using glib answers and clichés to respond verbally to social situations, he has also learnt the correct emotional responses and the expected ethical response in caring for others.

One afternoon when he was seven, he came home from school and announced that his good friend had been hospitalized for an accidental eye injury. I suggested that we should go that evening to visit his friend in the hospital. I thought he would be pleased with my idea, but to my consternation, he asked me a question I least expected: 'Why do we have to do that?'

'We need to show our love and concern, Aaron,' I replied. 'If you were the one in hospital, wouldn't you want your friends to visit you?'

Aaron was unable to respond spontaneously to a felt need. He needed an explanation to understand why it was only right to visit a sick friend. 'But are we the only ones who are going to visit him? Have my other friends visited him yet?' were his next questions. I knew he was expressing his reservation about being the only one among his classmates to visit the friend. That became more his concern than the fact that his friend's eye was seriously injured by a twig. Though he finally did agree to go, he did not exude the natural sympathy that a normal child would for a good friend.

On another occasion, there was a small commotion between him and his sister one night in their shared bedroom. Alysha was finding it hard to sleep and was calling out her brother's name softly to try to get his attention and sympathy. He reacted in anger and annoyance. As far as he was concerned, she was disturbing him and preventing him from sleeping. I entered the room to settle the little squabble. His sister was in tears. I told Aaron to show more concern for her. He immediately bowed down and prayed quietly by himself. My mum, who witnessed the scene, was impressed that Aaron responded with love and care for his sister. I chose to differ from her opinion. Knowing Aaron, I tend to believe that he was probably praying that his sister would stop disturbing him so that he could have his ten hours of sleep. He had learnt from his teacher in school that students need about ten hours of sleep. Since then, it had become 'law' to him. He would stop at nothing to ensure that he had the sleep that he needed, hence his agitation, which was blown out of proportion, when his schedule was disrupted.

Often he still poses the question 'Is he happy or sad?' whenever he sees someone crying. He has learnt that people usually cry when they are sad, and he accepts that a person can cry when overwhelmed with joy. But he can't tell one from the other. If a boy were to smile broadly to his classmates after being punished by his teacher, it would be too baffling and complex a response for him to grapple with.

Aaron comes across as being odd and eccentric because his emotional make-up runs against the grain of human nature.

How much more is the complexity of our human emotions an enigma, shrouded in complete mystery, for Aaron, who has no natural capacity to understand!

(b) Visual aversions, phobias, and hypersensitivities

It was something to behold, at least to me. For a while, I stood rooted to the ground, hardly believing what I was seeing: Aaron was enjoying himself with a few friends, revelling and squealing in delight while romping and stomping about in the mud. Another mother, especially one who is a no-nonsense neatness and cleanliness freak, might be appalled by the sight of her son smeared with smudges of mud all over the shirt, pants, and body. But I was thrilled beyond words. Knowing how Aaron was, with his natural aversion to mud, the incident marked a new milestone of achievement for him.

My mind flashed back two years prior to this incident, to another mud episode when he was five. After the therapy sessions in Giant Steps one day, I stopped to talk to his teacher while walking with Aaron towards the school gate. He walked on by himself, unaware that I was not next to him. Before I could even finish my sentence in my brief discourse, I heard a loud scream. As I had feared, it was Aaron. He had accidentally stepped into a puddle of thick muddy water. I rushed immediately to his rescue, but he continued to wail in terror, as if the mud were the most revolting and obnoxious of substances. In between his wild, reeling screams, he muttered and whined that it was my entire fault because I had stopped to talk to the teacher, hence my negligence in seeing to him.

To Aaron, mud was highly intolerable, considering his revulsion even to the smallest speck of dirt. He would reject any shirt or pants that had the minutest spot or stain.

With his uncanny mastery for detail, he could spot the most inconspicuous imperfection at one glance. He could not bring himself to wear any shirt or pants that did not pass the test of his scrutiny.

Taking Aaron for a walk at dusk could sometimes find Aaron running suddenly to seek cover behind a pillar, or he would close his eyes tightly while he walked. The reason? He had seen the moon before nightfall! To him, it was unnatural, for he associated the moon only with the darkness of the night. When the moon appeared while the sky was still bright, it did not conform to the rule or set pattern in his mind and was therefore abhorrent or even scary.

Aaron's paternal grandparents experienced a similar incident while driving Aaron and Alysha home from their house. Aaron suddenly saw the moon in the sky and began to cower in fear. When he was older, his grandfather explained to him about the various planets in the Milky Way and how the moon could also appear in the daytime. Since then, he had overcome his phobia.

One night I saw him curled up in a tight corner of his bed. I examined his bed sheet closely, expecting to find a stain on his bed, but there was none. He had avoided a part of his bed once before, as it had his bloodstain from a mosquito bite. But this time, I could see nothing extraordinary. When I asked him about it the next morning, he said that he would not like to sleep on a frog, the picture of which was in the middle of his bed sheet.

Another of Aaron's aversions was the sensation of getting wet. Woe betide him should just a few drops of rain suddenly fell on his head! So washing his hair at bath time was a constant tussle and a screaming match I had to put up with every day.

One day my family and I were enjoying a leisurely saunter by the beach. In a moment of blissful oblivion, we found ourselves walking closer to the edge of the beach. That unguarded moment was the killjoy of the day. Aaron soon felt a sensation of dampness in his shoes, and it triggered a huge tantrum. It started with just a whimper but soon ended with rage. Getting wet on any part of his body, even if it was a slight dampness, was repulsive to him. Seizing any means to pacify him, his dad rushed him to the public toilet and used the hand dryer to dry his shoes. Hilarious it might appear to the onlooker, but it did not matter in the least so long as it helped to assuage Aaron's anxiety and rage. It must have been the first and the last time that the hand dryer had been used to dry shoes!

The worst tension I had associated with Aaron's aversion to wetness was that he could not even stand his own tears. To make matters worse, his tearful outbursts were a daily affair, varying only in degree. Whenever he cried, his inconsolable tears added to his irritation and enraged him even more. It was a seemingly never-ending vicious cycle – his cries leading to a continuous stream of tears and his tears adding to the intensity of his cries. It was a daily gruelling grind for me, compounded by his incessant demand that I should stay by his side to wipe his tears. For my own sanity, my coping mechanism was to shut off and ignore his screams.

Aaron's revulsion to dirt and wetness extended to his sense of sight and imagination. Some scenes from children's videos were so repulsive to him that he would virtually cower in fear or run to take shelter. One was the scene of a plate of cream being poured onto the head of a man in a childish prank. Another was a poster advertisement promoting a certain brand of paper towel. To convey its effectiveness in cleaning any mess, the advertisement showed how the faces of some boys smeared with chocolate could be cleaned by it. Aaron was so repelled by the scene of the boys with such dirty faces that he avoided stepping into that shopping centre (which happened to be his favourite) for months, until the poster was removed and replaced by a new one.

While Aaron was devastatingly hypersensitive to dirt and wetness, he seemed to lack sensitivity in other areas which are second nature to normal children. He seemed not to be born with a built-in button/sensor to respond to any change of temperature in the weather. He followed rigidly the type of clothing that was expected for the season and had to be told if any adjustment was needed to accommodate a sudden change in weather. He would not be able to sense the need to put on or remove extra clothing in tandem with the temperature change.

Even regarding the sensation of hunger, it was all programmed by time and schedule; his mind would dictate when to feel the hunger pangs if it was past his mealtime and to feel full in the stomach if he had taken his usual portion of food.

Emotionally, he was paranoid about being laughed at. When someone laughed in his company, he always asked, 'Are you laughing at me?' (even when it had nothing to do with him). He had to be taught the difference between laughing *at* and laughing *with* him over an amusing situation. He would often overreact in a suspicious and brusque manner to anyone caught looking at him, be it intentional or unintentional. Even when he grew older, he was still self-conscious about anyone looking in his direction, except that he had learnt to be a little more civil, instead of walking away from the person in displeasure.

(c) Anxiety and panic disorders

*Do not be anxious about anything, but in
everything, by prayer and petition, with
thanksgiving, present your requests to God.*
—Phil. 4:6

I was meditating on the verse above and wondering when Aaron could ever internalize this verse and put it to practice. At age eleven, he was still unable to overcome anxiety in the most trite and unwarranted situation. I recall the following recent incident.

I was waiting for Aaron outside the school gate one afternoon. I saw him hobbling unsteadily towards the car. I guessed he must have injured his ankle. 'Mum, I have very bad news today,' he exclaimed in dismay as he entered the car. He prepared me for the worst. Then, as if petrified after committing a big crime, he reported in an alarming tone, 'I stepped on a bee, and I killed it!' What an anticlimax it turned out to be! I heaved a sigh of relief.

Unperturbed by the innocent accident, I glibly remarked, 'What's so bad about that, Aaron?'

'What?' he asked, as if in disbelief, shocked by my apparent disinterest in the matter. 'You mean killing a bee is not bad? You mean it's all right to kill animals?'

'Aaron, you eat meat, don't you? How would you get the meat if the animals had not been killed first?' I asked him in return, hoping to allay his fear and anxiety. But he was not pacified.

'I know I'm in deep trouble, Mum. When I killed the bee, the bee's friends were all around and they actually saw me doing it. Tomorrow, they will find me and sting me,' he lamented. His mind was highly imaginative and visual, and his illusive, illogical fear was very real to him. He was so overwhelmed by it that it rendered him stressed and helpless.

The seemingly insignificant incident of some bees flying around him at school precipitated a chain of events that triggered his state of distress. In trying to avoid the bees, he had accidentally stepped on one and even sprained his ankle. As a result, he was exempted from his swimming and athletic class. But missing any lesson was not such a straightforward matter to him. It meant a disruption to his normal schedule, upsetting his rigorous ritualistic adherence to routine and rules. It was enough to disorientate him altogether.

All the way back home from school, he nagged, fussed, and raved about the bee incident, the lessons he missed, and his sprained ankle. He continued his tirade of complaints incessantly, even after we'd been home for an hour. I reminded him to stop complaining and to do his homework or he would not be able to complete it in time. As he opened his school bag, he let out a loud cry. He was so muddled up and his mind so preoccupied about the whole episode that he had accidentally left his homework book in school.

Usually when something was amiss, he would look for a scapegoat (I was usually his whipping boy) so that he would not feel so bad about himself. He would be able to cope better if he knew that it was not his fault, even though he was intolerant about anything that went wrong. But in this case, he had no one else to blame except himself. Having an unrealistically high expectation of himself as being infallible, he could not stand making even the slightest slip or mistake. It was tantamount to breaking a moral law, and he could not excuse or tolerate this. Being punished the next day for not doing his homework was only next in gravity to the breaking of his own code of law. The incident was the culmination of the series of 'misfortunes' that befell him that day. It was the straw that broke the camel's back. His anxiety disorder caused a full-blown tantrum. He started to cry hysterically, as if his whole world had caved in. He railed about everything that had gone wrong that day. 'It's the worst day of my life. Why must everything bad happen to me? Nobody else is as unlucky as me. Why does God allow all these things to happen to me? Why must I be the only one to suffer? I know I'm in deep trouble ...' He went on chanting and ranting in between his plaintive cries.

Once started, his crippling anxiety and panic attacks knew no bounds. No amount of reasoning or distraction could pacify him. I tried telling him that his friends had previously left their homework behind without reacting the way he did. I told him that I would write a letter of explanation to his teacher so that he would not get into trouble. 'But ... but ...' He just continued crying, with a string of 'buts' and excuses and not wanting to listen to reason. I even told him that his bus usually arrived at school forty-five minutes before school began and that he had enough time to complete his homework. But his fatalistic attitude caused him to imagine the worst that could happen. 'But what if the doors aren't opened? I think the doors won't be opened so early and I won't have time to complete my homework. No, nothing can help. I know I am in deep, deep trouble ...' His disproportionate mental anguish overtook his ability to reason. He behaved like an inherent defeatist and pessimist.

Exhausted of ways to calm him, I had to leave him to cry and lament uncontrollably. After an hour, I told him to take his bath or he would be late for dinner. He did go upstairs, but after an hour, I became suspicious when he didn't come down. I went upstairs to check on him. I found him crying in the bathroom. He had tried to remove his undergarments before having his bath, but his aching ankle prevented him from doing so easily. He was again reminded about all that had happened, and he could not help wallowing in self-pity, anger, and depression. I helped him remove his clothes before he finally took his bath.

Putting up with Aaron's manic-depressive anxiety disorder occasionally is no mammoth task to me, having been seasoned by the frequency of those episodes in the past.

My mind flashed back to the days when he was impossible and his tantrums were almost a daily affair. He was an unrelenting order-and-routine freak. His peevish agitation and fury were easily provoked by something trivial, like a missing bookmark or a missing piece in a jigsaw puzzle. When he received a book, he checked every page to see that no page was missing. A missing page was so disturbing to him that he needed to write a disclaimer on the front inside-page of the book to explain it.

We used to experience some form of tension almost weekly on Sunday mornings. After church, my in-laws would go for lunch with us at the shopping centre. We went in two cars, one following the other. Aaron expected the two cars to stay together in the same sequence, one right behind the other, all the way to the shopping centre! As would often happen, other cars would come in between. With Aaron's eyes consistently looking through the back window of the car, the tension created each time the grandfather's car was missing from his sight was unnerving (his grandfather was an overly cautious slow driver).

Aaron's paternal grandparents had a rather eventful day when they took him to the Castle Hill shopping centre one Sunday afternoon after church. It was very crowded and to find an empty parking space in any of the levels was extremely difficult. When they finally found one, they happily parked there. Their joy was short-lived. Little did they expect to be greeted by Aaron's loud screams the moment they did so. They had absolutely no clue what the trigger was. In desperation, they called me on the phone. I immediately suspected that they had parked on the 'wrong' level. In Aaron's photographic mind, he had indelibly registered the level I parked the first time I took him there, and subsequently that was *the* one and only level to him. As if cast in stone, the set pattern could not be changed at any cost. Aaron's grandparents had no choice but to leave that precious parking spot in search for another at the 'right' level.

Fortunately, it did not take them too long to find one. However, it was hardly ten minutes later that I received another SOS call from them. They reported that Aaron started screaming all over again the moment they reversed the car backward into the parking spot. I suggested that they park the car differently, by driving forward into the parking spot instead, the way I usually did. It worked! Aaron's meltdown came to an immediate halt. What a relief for my in-laws at last.

When we went to a shopping centre as a family, together with his grandparents, no one was to wander off to do shopping on his or her own. He expected us to keep together as a complete group. Indeed, his obsession to set patterns and order permeated every facet of his life and inevitably restricted and controlled our movements.

There was an occasion when the grandparents left the church earlier on a Sunday morning and we had to break the habit of leaving the church together. While on the road, Aaron suddenly realized that the grandfather's car was not behind us. He was so alarmed and agitated by it that we had to summon the grandparents to go back to the church immediately. We too had to make a U-turn back to the church so that the two cars could start simultaneously from the church and leave sequentially, one behind the other, as was our usual practice after church.

He was nitpicky about every little thing that was not in accordance with the order he expected. As a toddler, seeing an incomplete pizza on the table with a piece missing was serious enough to trigger a tantrum.

During a vacation one time in Melbourne, Aaron and Alysha were left in the care of his paternal grandparents when my husband and I went out. Aaron was about five then. Feeling hungry, they brought a round meat pie home for lunch. When his grandmother cut it into pieces, Aaron was terribly upset. He could not stand seeing the pie being 'mutilated' into separate pieces. The pie must be seen as a complete whole and not get out of its regular shape. How the grandparents wished they had bought individual small round meat pies instead! They could have averted a hullabaloo.

One day when Aaron's grandfather was driving Aaron from Giant Steps to the grandparents' house, he decided to take a different route. Aaron suddenly burst out in fury and screamed like hell breaking loose. His grandfather was completely oblivious of what he had done to trigger it. He continued driving with Aaron screaming in the background. When he'd almost reached home, he suddenly heard Aaron uttering a word which meant that he should start the journey all over again. He got the message. He drove all the way back to Giant Steps and took the normal route home. Aaron could not have been pacified otherwise.

When he grew a little older, he had it fixed in his mind that his sister, being younger, must not be ahead of him in any activity, even if it was just finishing a meal or a drink. He was even obsessive compulsive about his sister getting out of bed in the morning earlier than he did. Even if she woke up earlier, she had to stay in bed until he got up.

He expected to be first in everything and a winner in any board game he played. Whenever he lost, he learnt gradually to cope with the undue stress by reminding himself that it was not a race or a competition. He also got uptight over any task or activity that was left half-done or incomplete. Once he started on anything, he had to make sure there was proper closure to the task. Whenever I faced a tight schedule or time constraint, I had to ensure that he did not start on anything he could not finish. His fixation about order and completion in every activity added untold stress to my life.

Aaron was advanced in his reading skills, even by the age of five. But his obsession about completing the task at one go often prevented him from wanting to begin reading a thick book. He had to be repeatedly reminded that it was all right to read a few chapters at a time. A bookmark at the right page, where he ended reading, finally did the trick. He was able to accept that his reading activity for that day had ended as denoted by the bookmark.

However, I did not expect another potential problem to surface as a result. A bookmark became so crucial a part of his unfinished book that it became an issue if it was missing or put back at the wrong page of the book. What I had been dreading happened one afternoon. 'Mum,' he screamed, panic-stricken and in tears, 'somebody took the bookmark from my storybook!'

'It doesn't matter, Aaron. Just continue reading the story from where you stopped,' I said.

'But I can't. Somebody did take away my bookmark, and I don't know where I stopped,' he whined and whimpered. He was completely unsettled and disoriented for the rest of the evening. After about half an hour, I could not tolerate his senseless tirade of blaming and complaining; I had to reprimand him, 'Stop putting the blame on others. Nobody would want to take your bookmark. It's your own carelessness, Aaron.'

That was it. He burst out in a greater torrent of tears and stormed out of the home library, screaming hysterically, 'You are now making me worse! You just don't understand! You make me cry even more; I can't stop these tears!' As mentioned, Aaron had an unnatural aversion to getting wet, and crying profusely only caused more tears to flow, thus wetting his face and shirt.

I lost my cool and yelled, 'Now stop that and stop thinking about yourself!'

'No, I can't. You know I can't stop thinking about it. I just can't …' He continued sobbing miserably.

Meanwhile, my family and I searched high and low for the missing bookmark. We ransacked the whole cupboard of books. We finally found it hidden among his other books. It must have dropped out of his book and gotten shuffled into a corner, behind his other book. What a relief for all of us!

However, the episode did not end there. Though he was glad to see the bookmark, the damage had been done and he needed time to get over it. He had to repeat the process of putting the bookmark back in the place where it was meant to be, at the exact page of the book. He then started all over again by taking the book from the shelf with the bookmark intact. Only then did he prepare himself to start reading the book, but not before his litany of complaints about the incident.

CHAPTER 9

BLACK-AND-WHITE PATTERNS OF COGNITIVE UNDERSTANDING

(a) Literal understanding of abstract concepts

I knew it was coming all along! When Aaron was about six, he suddenly confronted me with hard soul-searching questions, questions which I couldn't really answer: 'Why does God give me autism?' 'Will I still have autism when I grow up?' 'Why do I still have autism when I don't scream anymore?' He also asked some spiritually profound questions about God which he could not understand. When he read Bible stories, like the story of Abraham, for example, it blew his mind that God would ask Abraham to sacrifice his son Isaac just to test Abraham's faith. He proclaimed defiantly, 'I will disobey God if God tells me to kill Mum and Dad and says that He is testing me.'

He also could not fathom why innocent children had to die from natural disasters like tsunamis, forest fires, and earthquakes. They all defied his unflinching sense of order and social justice and were therefore very wrong in his eyes. It was also confusing and unjustifiable to him that his young uncle should turn blind after an operation for his tumour. In his black-and-white equation of social justice, no amount of explanation about God's nobler purposes could satisfy him and jolt him out of his sense of justice in the matter. He would continue to plague me endlessly with this question: 'But ... but ... why?' I finally brought the subject to an abrupt halt by distracting him with something that captivated his attention.

He also had difficulties understanding why God sometimes said no or to wait in answering prayers. This situation would usually emerge whenever he had a physical problem, be it pain or itch or any form of discomfort. He did not question God's love. To him, that was a given. What troubled him was reflected in the familiar refrain of his moaning, 'Why does God allow me to continue to suffer? I have prayed so many times the whole night, and I still have this pain in the morning. How many more times do I have to pray?' He also could not understand why God would still allow him to have his nose bleed or to get mosquito bites when he had prayed the night before for the Lord to protect him from them.

Aaron had a very low threshold for pain and suffering. It didn't help that his poor understanding of the concept 'wait' compounded this. His mind could only think in terms of simple equations of black and white. Any grey area would present a problem to him. The concept of time (and 'wait') constituted one of these grey areas. In the simplicity of his reasoning, it follows that 'God loves me; He hears my prayers, and He must answer them now.' Hence, he expected from God instant gratification for his complaints and needs.

An incident that happened in Canberra when he was about four showed clearly his intolerance for any delay that required him to wait. We drove to Canberra for a weekend holiday with my parents and stayed at an apartment. My husband and I were to renew our Malaysian passports at the Malaysian Embassy the following Monday morning, after which we had planned to journey home.

That morning, however, my mum went to Aaron's room and engaged him in a casual chat, little expecting that it would blow up into a big tantrum for Aaron. She didn't know that she had said the wrong thing when she mentioned going home that day. It had immediately registered in Aaron's mind that it was time to go home, and he was ready to leave the very next minute. We tried to explain to him that he had to wait for his dad and me to get the passports renewed first, but he didn't listen. Having no concept of time and 'wait', whatever was said made no sense to him. He'd already made up his mind, and nothing could change that – no amount of coaxing and reasoning. His fury ascended to its peak just when his dad and I had to leave for the embassy and he was left behind with his grandparents. Did they have a hard time putting up with his violent temper and frenzy! I could see how tense they had been and how relieved they were to see us back at the apartment an hour later. Aaron finally calmed down when we started our journey home.

Aaron's poor understanding of time made him very confused with terms like 'soon', 'wait for a while', 'afterwards', and 'later'. He would always check after a little while and say, 'Is it now?' A specific length of time must be spelt out clearly to him if he were expected to wait. With that, he would not make any fuss or complaint, even if it was for a long time.

Besides 'wait', his simplistic way of thinking had no place for figurative expressions and words with hidden nuances of meaning. They presented another obvious grey area to him. When he was about four, I used to remark that my ears were bursting because he was screaming so loudly. When I said that, he would immediately rush to cup my ears with his palms to prevent that from happening literally. He also shocked me one day by asking a rather preposterous question: 'Mum, does your memory have money?'

My immediate reaction: 'What on earth are you asking about, Aaron?' Then I remembered that I had just made a casual remark about having a poor memory. To Aaron, 'poor' meant only one thing – not having enough money. He asked the question because his literal interpretation of 'poor memory' just didn't add up or make any sense to him.

Once we were travelling on a long journey in Malaysia, and Aaron and Alysha were making a lot of noise in the car, playing their own games. I told them to quieten down, as their grandfather was concentrating on his driving and added that too much noise could cause him to lose his way. Immediately, Aaron stopped his game and, getting all alarmed, asked, 'Are we lost now?' He repeated the question every now and then. We had to assure him that we were not lost yet. He took every word that was said literally and without question.

When he was about eight, we were having lunch at a food court when his dad told him, 'Aaron, let's go to the NIKE shop afterwards. Finish your lunch quickly and follow me.' When he had finished his lunch, his dad got up and happened to scratch his head. Aaron got up and did exactly what his dad did, scratching his own head. 'Not that,' said his dad, and with a sense of humour, he quickly took him by the hand to the Nike shop without a chuckle. I had to stifle my laughter, for I knew that he would be ultra sensitive if he saw anyone laughing at him. Obviously, he didn't understand that scratching his head was not meant to be part of his father's instructions.

Being very literal, Aaron found it difficult to draw conclusions through the process of induction, deduction, or inference from any facts given. For example, if there was a story about a cat chasing a mouse and it ended with the statement that the cat had a satisfying meal, he would not be able to deduce that the cat had eaten the mouse, for it was not stated specifically.

Aaron was a poor mind reader and lacked the ability to understand and predict behaviour. He could not read the non-verbal cues of others and was thus not privy to the emotions, desires, perceptions, intentions, or mental states of others.

One day, while watching the musical *Hairspray*, he had to ask his younger sister why she laughed when the actress put a ring on her own ring finger while daydreaming of her boyfriend. He obviously had no idea what that implied. There was yet another occasion when his dad asked if he would like to use the same cup as his friend's for his drink. He appeared flabbergasted; he thought that it meant sharing the same cup with his friend when his dad meant using the same *kind* of cup.

Because of his naivety, he can still be easily tricked or taken for a ride. On one occasion, our family went on a holiday together with my friend's family. My friend's son, Joshua, wanted to drink the last box of chocolate milk that was in the fridge. His mother told him that he could only do so if Aaron didn't want any. Joshua took the box from the fridge and asked, 'Aaron, can I drink this box of chocolate milk?'

Aaron, puzzled and unable to infer Joshua's intention, was irritated and asked impetuously, 'If you want to drink it, why do you have to ask me? How do I know whether you want to drink the chocolate milk or not?' Aaron, as was his usual problem, could not read Joshua's mind. Joshua, smugly satisfied with Aaron's response, took it to mean that Aaron did not want any, and he gleefully gulped down the drink. Actually, the chocolate milk was one of Aaron's favourites. If his friend had asked him a more direct question, like 'Do you want to drink this?' Aaron would have said yes.

Nor could Aaron pick up skills easily by merely observing others and then applying them to himself. He found it hard to put himself in someone else's shoes. The skills he learned in his mind would remain a theory if he had not felt and learnt them empirically. The theory and practical part of his learning were divorced as separate units and were not perceived as integral parts of the whole. To Aaron, translating the theoretical knowledge in his mind into practice in real life was a huge task. For instance, he could not naturally pick up the simple skill of sitting on a swing by watching how others did it. He would be dumbfounded when asked to sit on the swing himself. He had to be taught experientially before he could swing on it.

Aaron looking lost at the playground

As Aaron often stumbled over figurative indirect statements or questions, it was hardly surprising that the questions he asked were also extremely predictable and straightforward. He had to be trained to ask inference and other helpful questions that help draw out information. In one of his therapy sessions, he was shown a picture of Santa Claus riding on a sleigh, driven by reindeers and carrying boxes of presents. When told to ask questions to elicit information, he could only manage some kindergarten-level questions: 'Does the reindeer have a tail?' and 'Does it have ears?' It was only at the end of the session that he finally succeeded in asking some helpful fact-finding questions: 'Where is Santa going?' and 'What's in the boxes?'

Aaron has made much progress in understanding many words and expressions in their non-literal context. By the age of seven, he had also learnt expressions for social interactions, such as 'I'm sorry to inform you' and 'It's none of your business.' I could not help being amused when he sometimes used these expressions inappropriately. Being literal, he used the expressions indiscriminately, be it in a formal or informal context. He reported to me one day, 'I'm sorry to inform you, Mum, that Dad didn't answer my question.' He'd simply asked his dad when he should stop reading his storybook, and his dad probably didn't hear him, being absorbed in his work.

On another occasion, he surprised all his friends with the most succinct remark: 'It's none of your business, Angela' when he told Angela off for teasing one of his friends. His brave and apt remark in standing up for his friend got him so much applause from his friends that he felt elated and happy the whole of that day. It gave him the affirmation he needed.

He also understood many figurative expressions, although it was still bewildering for him to grasp that being the 'apple of one's eye' meant being someone that one is fond of. He had also improved greatly in the area of making assumptions which used to be a bit of an enigma to him. He found it hard to imagine things that didn't really happen.

Today (at age eleven), however, he can manage an imaginative composition – for example, of life as an astronaut. However, he still has a compulsive need for set patterns in the processing of his thoughts. He thinks visually and hence his handicap in analysing abstract ideas. Making logical conclusions of information through the process of induction, deduction, and inference will always be a challenge to him.

Being strictly black and white in the way he views things, he sees no lies and tells no lies. He is too candidly straightforward, truthful, and naive to be capable of anything naughty, furtive, or sly just to get out of trouble. Trickery and shrewdness are foreign to his nature. Though truthfulness is a virtue, on the negative side, he can easily fall prey to any trickster, prankster, liar, or deceiver. Lacking discernment, he takes in lock, stock and barrel what is said, irrespective of who said it. His naivety and trusting nature make him an easy victim of practical jokes. Taking any joke too literally and seriously, he is likely to overreact to something that is meant to be just clean fun. Consequently, he may appear to be a spoilsport who lacks a good sense of humour, when in fact he doesn't catch the twist in the joke. It may not match his simple black-and-white equation, and unless explained to him, a joke will usually fall flat on him.

On the other hand, he is so truthful about everything that he does not understand that some truths are better left unsaid. For example, he had no qualms explaining why his sister was sent home from school when she had head lice. He lacked the social gumption to pretend or withhold uncomfortable or embarrassing information. Hence, most of his disrespectful and inconsiderate remarks or actions stem from ignorance and naivety. He does not know any better but to give a direct answer to any question asked.

His theory of mind deficits could baffle typical ordinary people and explain much of his learning, social, and communicative impairments. Hopefully, his fragile self-esteem will not be dented by those who make him the brunt of their cruel jokes.

(b) Time issues

The concept of time had been confusing to Aaron because it was not something visible and tangible. He loved timetables (schedules), as they represented visible maps of time, like a frame that made time comprehensible in terms of the relationship between the ways different activities change. They showed him when everything was going to happen and thus gave him a sense of security and calmness. Things or incidents that were unexpected, unfamiliar, or unprecedented often precipitated an anxiety disorder or panic attack in him. Timetables acted like his safety valve and enabled him to accept the expected changes in activities denoted by time.

Aaron's timetable, be it written or imaginary, was an asset to him, but it also became a bane of his life as he grew too attached to it. His unflinching adherence to it made it a monster that dictated his life. It created untold tension for my family and me. He was happy and at peace with himself and the world if there was no disruption to his normal schedule, but the probability of that happening was very slim. To expect such unrealistic absolutes and ideals were to expect the impossible. A myriad of unpredictable incidents upset the tabulated schedule and afflicted him with great anxiety. Even his grandparents arriving at our home unannounced was a disruption, especially when he was in the midst of writing in his journal. Furthermore, he had developed the obsessive habit of always checking the time before and after each activity, just to be sure that he kept rigorously to his timetable.

A slow motion rerun of past incidents associated with the issue of time wafted through my mind. Most of these incidents happened during the following times: Sunday mornings (on the way to church), mealtimes, and bedtimes.

One Sunday morning when we were running a little late on our way to church, Aaron got unduly anxious. 'Oh, it's already nine fifty-two!' Aaron cried out frantically as he looked at the digital clock in the car. 'We're going to be late! I don't want to be late. We cannot reach the church at ten o'clock. No, no, why must we be late?'

I tried to calm him down. 'Aaron, we're not really late. Even if we are a few minutes late, it's all right. Your friends Joshua and Hannah often come later than you, and they do not fuss about it.'

'But ... but ... I don't want to be late. I'm sure Joshua and Hannah are already there,' he lamented repetitively, refusing to be consoled. His observing the seconds and minutes ticking by made everyone tense and worked up. The tension in the atmosphere mounted with his continuous barrage of nagging, complaining, whingeing, fussing, pleading, and blaming all the time.

It often happens that the more you're in a hurry, the more you meet the unavoidable, with Murphy's Law coming into play. In our haste, we sometimes made a careless slip or a wrong turn which resulted in causing further delay. The rest of the day would be marred for him and for us.

Mealtimes could also create a tension for us. Aaron had his fixed schedule for meals – breakfast, morning tea, lunch, afternoon tea, and then dinner. Even when we were more relaxed and flexible about meals during our vacation, he still expected all five meals to be served – and in sequential order. To skip morning tea and only have lunch after a late heavy breakfast would be only natural. But to Aaron, lunch must be preceded by morning tea. Knowing how inflexible he was, I had to recall quickly any small thing he had taken prior to lunch, be it a drink or a biscuit, and then convince him that it was his morning tea. It seemed so silly because, for once, I could think of nothing else to say except that the vitamin pills that he had taken was his morning tea. How relieved I was when he accepted my explanation that the vitamins were a food supplement and could thus serve as his morning tea.

Besides expecting to have his five meals in that sequential order, he had also established his own timetable for the meals, which must be adhered to rigidly; lunch must be taken by two in the afternoon and dinner by eight in the evening. Any delay in the time would inject such tension into his nerves that he could turn pale and literally tremble in fear and trepidation.

During our vacation in Malaysia, it was hard to keep strictly to a tight schedule. After a swim one evening, it was almost 7.30 p.m. when we got ready to go for dinner. Knowing how Aaron was, we had to rush to the nearest restaurant, but to our dismay, it was crowded and we had to wait for a table. In the meantime, Aaron was eyeing the clock and becoming increasingly tense by the minute. If only we could jump the queue to have our turn first. We were only seated by 7.45 p.m.

By 7.53 p.m., he was not just complaining incessantly; he was also in tears. He was already getting out of control when, in between sobs, he cried out as if in despair, 'I'm starving! Why don't they care? Why don't they bring the food now? Why did we have to come this late? Why did we have to come to this restaurant …?' His tension accelerated, and his intense emotions got us all worked up. His dad tried a quick fix by rushing to the nearest department store to get some cookies. He tried to convince Aaron that this was his entrée, but the trick did not work, as Aaron insisted that it was not part of his dinner. He portrayed such a picture of starvation that my friend who was with me was taken in and really believed that he had severe hunger pangs. I explained to her that the intensity of his reaction was exaggerated and that it was his excuse to get the food immediately so his mealtime rule would not be broken.

Thank God the food arrived in the nick of time. He hurriedly put one morsel of food into his mouth. It meant that he had commenced his dinner in time and he was 'saved'. He was instantly back to his normal self. Since that experience, I had a contingent plan should mealtime be delayed. I ensured that there was always some kind of food in my bag, just in case.

Another episode that also took place in Malaysia saw my dad driving recklessly to reach home one night, just to beat the time, for the sake of Aaron's bedtime. This happened on a night we went for dinner at my brother's home, about twenty kilometres away from my parents' apartment. We started the dinner late, as we had to wait for some friends to come. They happened to have a flight delay. After dinner, we spent some time chatting and clearing up while the children played by themselves. When we decided to go home, we did not realize that it was already 11.30 p.m.

When Aaron got into the car, he cried out in alarm when he saw the time on the digital clock. 'Oh no, it's already eleven thirty-five. I must be in bed before midnight.' Only then did it dawn on us the seriousness of the lateness of the hour. It would take at least half an hour on the road to reach my parents' apartment.

Aaron's eyes glued to the clock all along the way was certainly of no help. We tried to distract him, but there was no way we could keep him from focusing on the minutes ticking by. He got more tensed and alarmed with each passing minute. The only thing that provided us with some relief from his persistent repetitive ranting was the plaza toll, which caught his attention for a minute or two.

My dad drove as he had never driven before. For once, he threw caution to the wind and raced against time, knowing what it would mean for Aaron if we arrived home after midnight. At best, he would be unreasonable and inconsolable. At his worst, he could be beside himself in his bizarre reaction. In the meantime, Aaron just could not be pacified. He got louder and increasingly desperate and panicky. We tried to cover the digital clock but it was of no use. No amount of reasoning or explanation could get him out of his fixation regarding sleeping before twelve. Passing midnight, to him, meant that it was already another day and he would have missed his sleep for one whole day. It might sound absurd to anyone else, but to Aaron it was no laughing matter. To us who were with him, the urgency of the moment and of every second that passed was so tense and crucial that it could drive any person with a weak heart to an untimely heart attack.

We drove past the gate of our apartment just before the stroke of midnight. It was a ludicrous sight to see all of us dashing from the lift into the apartment. It was like a matter of life and death. The moment we got into the apartment, Aaron was rushed into his room and put straight into bed, without having his nightcap, brushing his teeth, or even changing into his pyjamas. The lights were turned off immediately. I had convinced Aaron that he was in bed a second before midnight! The whole incident reminded me of the Cinderella story, in which midnight was the defining moment for the magic of the night to be broken. In Aaron's case, at the chime of twelve, he would be robbed of one day's sleep, as if a magic spell had been broken. The difference is that this was no fairy tale.

Poor Alysha, who had to go to bed together with her brother, was left utterly lost and confused. 'But I haven't changed or brushed my teeth yet,' she complained. We ignored her complaints. She had to comply with her brother's less-than-normal behaviour and was obligated to go to sleep without having changed into her pyjamas. Alysha had learnt to put up with her brother's peculiarities even when she least understood.

The half-hour nightmarish roller-coaster trip back home was a ride that we will never ever forget. Thank God we did not get into problems with the law when we sped all the way and once even beat the traffic light. Not only that – it was also a miracle indeed that nothing untoward happened, for my dad had to concentrate intensely in the darkness of the night with his less-than-perfect night vision.

In tandem with Aaron's obsession in keeping time, his watch became his indispensable possession. One day he carelessly left it behind at his grandparents' house and only realized it when we had arrived home. As if he had lost part of himself, he started badgering me to go back to his grandparents' house to recover the watch. Feeling worn out by a full day's busy schedule, I was not prepared to brave the traffic jam that night just to retrieve the watch, so I braced myself for the worst to happen. He pleaded and hollered mournfully, but I stood my ground. In between his torrent of wailing and tears, he blurted out something that struck a chord in my heart: 'You just cannot understand that the watch is so important to me. You don't even understand that I have autism!' I was jolted for a moment by his heartbreaking remark. It touched me deeply that he realized he was different and that he couldn't help himself. He behaved like one suffering from the withdrawal symptoms of a drug addiction. I was so tempted to give in, to ease his highly strung anxiety, but I decided to stand firm. I shared his gruelling pain as he took hours to grieve over the absence of his watch that night.

It was a tough decision that I made that night, but I believe that at times it is kind to be cruel. A short-term gain could be a long-term pain, and vice versa. He did gradually overcome his compulsive need for a watch and his obsession in checking the time every now and then. Today a watch to him is something nice to have but not a must-have and he doesn't need to wear one to school.

(c) Concept of space

I read about Abraham Lincoln having a great sense of humour. His humour helped him bear the strain and pressure he faced as president during the American Civil War. Laughing at himself kept him from becoming defensive, and he could sometimes win over an opponent with a good story spiked with a wholesome sense of humour.

If only Aaron has a good sense of humour, it would certainly help him handle many ludicrous situations resulting from his funny out-of-the-ordinary behaviour at times. It evokes a spontaneous outburst of humour in some, a look of curiosity or unbelief in others, and in some others, a look of disgust or disapproval. How I wish Aaron could laugh at himself at such times instead of withdrawing into his own world of bashfulness and feeling a little like an alien on planet Earth.

Aaron has no concept of space, and his deficiency in this area landed him in some amusing outcomes. An episode that is still vivid in my mind happened at a bus stop one day. I took him and Alysha to the bus stop where they would catch their bus to school. There was a boy seated on the bench at the bus stop. The next thing I knew, Aaron had plonked himself closely next to the boy and was pushing the boy into a tight corner. The poor boy sidled to the extreme end of the bench, possibly feeling uneasy about it. Aaron didn't even realize that he was doing something socially unacceptable by not giving the boy any comfortable breathing space in between. He, in fact, thought he was being considerate by creating the maximum space for others, including his sister and me, to sit down on the bench.

No one in his normal senses would choose to sit in such close proximity to a total stranger unless that was the only space left on the bench. It looked totally out of place and unnatural. Fortunately, the boy was civil, cool, sporting, and made no outward fuss, though I believe he must have been nonplussed and wondering what Aaron was up to.

I dread to think what it would have been like if he had been a few years older and the student next to him happened to be a girl. It would have been most embarrassing, but Aaron would ironically be the last person to realise it. His innocent gesture could have been misconstrued as overtures of a precocious streetwise young lad attempting to make advances on a young lass. And stretching the imagination a little further, she might cringe in fear or flee in terror, or both, if she happened to be extremely alarmed by it – and all over an innocuous act of pure innocence, born out of an inborn counter-normal concept of 'non-space'.

Until I understood Aaron's problem, his odd behaviour also left me confounded. His world view of space was unlike our normal one. From Aaron's point of view, it was absolutely the most logical and sensible thing to do – to sit next to the boy without leaving any space in between. To him, that was his legitimate place and the rest of the space left on the bench was reserved for other students, whether they were going to be there or not. He didn't know any better. His one-size-fits-all concept dictated his action. In this case, he had to learn the importance of flexibility and allowing for personal physical space instead of fixing his mind on reserving the space for some phantom students who were unlikely to appear.

Aaron's deficiency was not just confined to physical space; he also did not understand one's need for personal private space. Unless he was told, he was oblivious of what intrusion into one's privacy really meant. Perceiving all things in terms of either black or white, the need for personal space was irrelevant or unknown to him.

One day his sister was writing a composition, and Aaron, having finished his homework, was just hanging around her and peering occasionally at what she was writing. Annoyed and irritated by his intrusion, she started yelling at him. He reacted in confusion and anger. He could not understand that his action was an intrusion into her privacy, as he did not expect his sister to have anything to hide from him. After all, he himself was like an open book; whatever he had written was open for her or for anyone else to read. He had never thought that it was any private matter, unless it was meant to be a secret.

Having no concept of space, it is inevitable that Aaron would, at one time or another, get into problems and be misunderstood as a result. Knowing him, he would have no qualms, for example, in entering anyone's room or office at any time, when faced with a pressing need, unless he had been told not to do so specifically. If he was told to stick closely to a friend who could help see to his needs, the likelihood was that he might literally follow him closely all around, thus suffocating his poor friend with his very presence. He might not know when to give his friend the private and social space his friend needed unless it was clearly and meticulously spelt out to him. The skill to respect the personal space of others did not come naturally to him. What is mere common sense to us is certainly 'uncommon' sense to him!

CHAPTER 10

STRENGTH AND WEAKNESS IN SKILLS

(a) Unique talent in calculation

'Mum, when will we be going for our holidays in Malaysia?' Aaron asked me out of the blue one day.

'We'll be going in June. Why, Aaron?' I asked, curious that he should suddenly pop that question since June was several months away.

'But, mum,' he continued, 'I need to know exactly the date when we will be leaving.'

'It's on the twenty-sixth of June,' I said, not knowing what was on his mind.

'Oh, then it's all right. It's on a Saturday,' he muttered, as if to himself.

I guessed from his response that he just wanted to be sure that he didn't miss any of his school days or activities, being a stickler for rules. Then it suddenly occurred to me that he could tell the day without even casting a glance at the calendar. 'How do you know that the twenty-sixth of June is a Saturday? Did you have a look at the calendar earlier?' I asked in surprise.

'No,' he replied in a serious tone, devoid of any guile.

'Then how did you know it was a Saturday?' I quizzed again.

'I just know,' he answered matter-of-factly.

My curiosity aroused, I casually tested him on some other dates from that year, the past year, and the following year, not expecting him to know the answers. He gave me the answers immediately. When I later checked the calendar, I was astounded to find that he could tell me with absolute accuracy the days corresponding to the dates asked. It was certainly no fluke shot, as he had not spent time perusing or studying the calendar prior to this. It was unbelievable! At the age of six, his mind was able to compute, within seconds, the days from any dates given and from any year. I had accidentally stumbled upon an amazing discovery of a gift he had. On top of it, he even had all the leap years taken into consideration, lest anyone should trip him up on the date, February 29. How he did it was anybody's guess. It came so naturally to him that it was as if he had an inbuilt computer to do it. In fact, he thought others were like him, and he was oblivious of the fact that it was a rare feat peculiar to very few, like him.

One day Aaron's dad did manage to unravel the mystery of how his mind worked. Aaron shared confidentially with his dad that he had devised a formula which was the handy tool that he used. It was based on repetitive patterns of certain months in a year and of the different years as well. However, without a gifted photographic memory like Aaron's, it would be highly laborious and painstaking to master the skill.

I could not contain my excitement at discovering his supernatural gift. I shared the news with family members and close friends. Soon he became like a little sensational celebrity within family circles. Those who heard about it wanted to test him out for themselves. They came away from it feeling amused, amazed, and thrilled that a small boy was capable of something they had absolutely no clue about. Filled with a sense of wonder, they could only conclude that it was something out of this world!

However, it did not take long for Aaron to realize that he was 'different' and that he had been 'used' to showcase that which marked his uniqueness. It was not something he enjoyed doing, nor was it something he was very proud of. He grew increasingly sensitive and even suspicious about the way everyone tried to test him about dates. He started to withdraw whenever he sensed the limelight focusing on him. Soon the oft-repeated request had to be encapsulated in different creative forms to ward off his suspicion. Tact and discretion became necessary to trick him into complying – that is, only if he was convinced of the valid reason that he had to do so. He chafed at the unnecessary attention he was receiving, and with time he grew increasingly reluctant to reveal his hidden talent. What any child would enjoy celebrating and exhibiting as an unusual gift became, to him, a bane or a burden. He fought shy of being abnormal and would trade anything to be normal and ordinary. His acute inherent sensitivity about being 'special' caused him to consciously retreat to the background. He soon learnt to put up with the pressure of displaying his skill by resorting to the strategies of silence, nonchalance, or an outright answer: 'I don't know!'

One day, however, he surprised us when he obliged to give the answer when a relative asked him about a certain date important to her. We were taken aback when the answer he gave that day was wrong. We had hitherto taken for granted that his mind, like a human computer, was infallible, and the slight miss that day caught us all gawking at him in disbelief. It was certainly not like him to make any mistake. On the other hand, Aaron was totally unruffled, nor was he perturbed about it. Making no excuses for himself, he responded gingerly, as if with a declaratory statement of triumph, 'That means I'm normal.' It was a touching statement to me. It spoke of his deep desire and quest to be normal. He seemed to be proclaiming his day of liberty: free to be ordinary and free from being singled out to demonstrate his extraordinariness. Since then, our enthusiasm of tricking him to tell waned to the point of its natural demise.

Aaron's unique ability manifested itself for only about a year or so. Could this supernatural endowment have come and gone within such a short span of time, like a passing spark of brilliance? Could it have naturally turned rusty through lack of use or through deliberateness? Or could Aaron have chosen the path of least resistance by repressing, suppressing, and burying his talent as his defence mechanism for unwarranted attention? Nobody knows. Not even Aaron. Ask Aaron and his standard answer will probably be 'I don't know.' Only God knows.

(b) Weak gross motor skills

Aaron is not naturally endowed with good motor skills. During his preschool days, it was so painful to me to see him struggling even to kick a ball forcefully. His inadequacy in muscular coordination and motor skills robbed him of the fun and thrill that other children, especially boys, enjoyed in physical activities. His clumsiness in jumping, kicking, hopping, and essentially movements involving his limbs always caused him to lag behind in outdoor games and sports. I feared that his shortcoming would make him an easy target of ridiculing, sneering, intimidation, and even exclusion by his less considerate and tolerant friends. Any manner of teasing shown, intentional or unintentional, could drive a wedge between him and his friends, causing him to withdraw even more into his own world.

Despite his limitations, Aaron's dad, being a keen sportsman himself, did not give up hope that, with the right kind of coaching, Aaron could emerge out of his natural handicap and even arrive at excellence in some sports. I, being more realistic, however, was less hopeful. My highest expectation for him was that he might achieve mediocrity in perhaps a few events. My more reasonable dream would, I thought, spare me of any disappointment in the future.

Aaron had to face his first major challenge when he was eight, in Year Two in the mainstream school. Like all other students in the school, he had to complete a two-kilometre cross-country run. With no prior training or experience in long-distance running, I doubted that he had the stamina to run that distance. To be unable to complete the race was no simple matter to Aaron. That was the crux of my concern. Unlike other boys who would possibly laugh it off, it would be devastating for him if he could not complete what he had started. His obsession was such that he could not cope with any unfinished business. It was tantamount to courting a disaster serious enough to trigger a tidal wave of emotions.

I decided to devise a strategy that I hoped could alleviate the problem. I gave him specific instructions to follow. I told him to take it easy and to walk or jog slowly at the same pace all the way. He was to ignore his friends who might begin running very fast and who could be far ahead of him. I knew that an accelerated pace right from the start of the race could easily exhaust him; a constant pace, on the other hand, would ensure a better chance for him to complete the race.

I was cheering him on during the initial one hundred metres from the starting point. Following my instructions became his primary goal in the race. He was so focused on it that he kept asking me all the time, while I was there, if he had been consistent in his pace.

Aaron was excellent in complying with my instructions. He was completely oblivious of his friends, who raced ahead of him at the beginning. As it was a very hilly terrain, many of them became exhausted and stopped to rest on the way. Aaron just continued jogging steadily past them and was unperturbed by them or any other distraction. When he finally neared the finishing line, he didn't make a dash for it. He glided past the finishing line with amazing ease, like a seasoned marathon runner. He didn't look in the least exhausted and was not even panting like most of the other boys. In fact, he looked fit enough to continue another kilometre or so.

My heart leapt for joy to see that Aaron had actually done it – and with excellence too. He was among the first ten students to complete the race! If Aaron himself did not feel a sense of accomplishment, I did. I was secretly congratulating myself for the right modus operandi I gave him. It worked, and to think that Aaron had beaten all odds to come this far gave me hope that he might still have hidden potential yet to be tapped.

As for Aaron, it didn't matter in the least how he fared. He was not brimming with pride, nor was he overwhelmed with excitement at his good performance. All that mattered to him was that he had completed a task he had set for himself. To me, his feat was like a graphic moral display of the fable 'The Tortoise and the Hare' and the proverb 'Slow and steady wins the race'.

Having overcome the first hurdle, I was more hopeful that he would overcome the next, which, to me, was even more challenging. Since his toddler days, his natural aversion to water would, I feared, be his greatest deterrent to pick up swimming. If just a few drops of rain on his head could drive him into a frenzy, I wondered how he could ever put his head underwater. Despite my little faith, I sent him for swimming lessons when he was five, having forewarned the special needs coach about Aaron's shortcomings and phobia.

The coach was prepared to take Aaron through painstaking baby steps of learning the skill as well as help him overcome his phobia. Thankfully, Aaron was a cooperative and conscientious learner. Being a meticulous follower of instructions certainly helped.

Aaron had to begin his first lesson by walking along the side of the pool and just getting his feet wet. He then learnt to wade in the water during the next few lessons. Each lesson was a baby step to get Aaron to go deeper into the water, from the leg level to the knee and then to the waist. Though he progressed at a snail speed, he was learning to overcome his phobia. It was only a year later that he could put his head under the water. That was the greatest milestone of progress for him. He overcame his initial resistance at that point. With the help of the coach, his perseverance paid off. After about two years, he managed to master the breaststroke. Learning other styles after that required relatively less effort on his part. Seeing how it all began, his progress was remarkable, to say the least.

In Year Three, he emerged second for his year in the breaststroke event in the swimming carnival organised by the school. It marked the turning point of his swimming career. A year later, he was first in the freestyle event. In Year Five, when he was transferred to an elite private school, he achieved first place for his backstroke. Since then, swimming, the sport that I was most apprehensive about for Aaron, had turned out to be his forte.

At the award presentation ceremony at his school, Aaron was perhaps the coolest boy, acting completely unexcited. My mind flashed back to Aaron's final year in Giant Steps, when he and another girl were chosen to read a few sentences on the stage. It was a proud moment for all of us as we remembered how he started with no words or language. Aaron exuded unwavering confidence and had no stage fright at all. It was as if he was emotionally rather detached from the audience. This time, however, he was a little self-conscious. Going up on the stage to receive any award was not what Aaron looked forward to, as he never enjoyed attention and acclamation. He was not at all brimming with pride like most award winners. He was more concerned and excited about the type and colour of the ribbon on the trophy, and the number written on it, than the actual award itself!

As I reminisced about Aaron's remarkable progress, especially in swimming, I felt the words of Jesus, addressed to the disciples on the road to Emmaus, speaking to me: 'How foolish you are, and how slow of heart to believe' (Luke 24:25).

CHAPTER 11

RANDOM EVENTS AT AGE ELEVEN

B y the age of eleven, Aaron had overcome many of his challenges. To a casual observer, he was anything but 'abnormal'. The random events, like snapshots of him in various settings, would reveal some of his remaining innate limitations.

1. Being literal and not lateral

(i) At his maternal grandparents' house (in Malaysia)

Aaron was engrossed in a game of chess with his sister when his grandmother asked if he would like to have some 'love letters' for tea. His immediate response: 'No, thanks, I don't eat love letters.' Knowing that his sister loved this traditional Chinese pastry, his grandmother placed some of the love letters on a plate in front of them. To her surprise, Aaron was the one who was helping himself lavishly to them. He obviously enjoyed eating them. Confused, she asked me quietly about the apparent contradiction in Aaron's actions. The fact that Aaron's words did not match his actions was no paradox to me. He had just understood the term 'love letters' literally. He was either too engrossed in the game to make a logical deduction of the word or it was a mere indication of his natural instinctive thinking pattern. He was probably completely oblivious of the confusion he had caused.

(ii) In church (at Easter service)

The pastor gave an invitation at the end of the service for those who wished to be 'reconciled to God' to go forward for prayer. Aaron was about to move from his seat when I stopped him. 'Aaron, you have prayed to receive Christ, and you are a Christian. You don't need to go forward.'

'But does that mean that I am already reconciled to God?' he asked very seriously.

'Of course, Aaron,' I answered.

Not convinced, he asked again, 'Are you sure?'

Aaron takes his faith very seriously. Each time an altar call is made from the pulpit, he wants to go forward, as he takes the pastor's words literally. It isn't surprising, then, that he has walked up to the front for prayer more than once, just to be sure.

(iii) At home watching TV

'Master Chef' has been my family's favourite program on TV. Gathered around the TV while enjoying our dinner, we derive much pleasure and thrill watching the ingenuity of amateur cooks whipping up delicious dishes within a set time and using the ingredients given.

One night we noticed that 'Master Chef for Kids' would soon be introduced; applications were open. Aaron, seeing that he was eligible in age to apply, asked me a serious question without giving it a second thought, 'Mum, I'm eligible. Shall I apply for it?'

My immediate response to his preposterous question was, 'Aaron, you have never tried cooking, and you know nothing about cooking. How can you apply?'

Any other kid in his position would not have even considered applying for it!'

2. Inept social expressions

(i) Arriving home after a few days away at the school camp, he blurted out a forthright straightforward confession: 'No offence, Mum, but I didn't think of you at all during the camp.'

(ii) While watching a TV show, he surprised me with a remark: 'Oh, sexy.' I was sure he was innocently oblivious of the implication of the word, for the modestly dressed, genteel girl on the TV that he had referred to was far from what the word would suggest.

'What does sexy mean, Aaron?' I asked him, expecting to have a little laugh over his ludicrous understanding of the word. Instead, he challenged me with a question.

'What? Don't you know the meaning of the word?' I am still baffled as to what his understanding of the word is.

3.   Being overanxious

My husband and I were so deeply engrossed in our interesting conversation with friends during a dinner that we forgot all about the time. We had left Aaron and his sister at their grandparents' house. It was past eleven that night when Aaron called me anxiously on my mobile phone. He was brief and to the point: 'Mum, are we staying over at Kong Kong and Ma Ma's house, or are you coming soon to pick us up?' We had not planned for them to sleep over, but as it was already very late, my husband decided there and then that they should sleep over in the grandparents' home. 'Oh,' he exclaimed, 'but don't forget to pick me up for my soccer practice tomorrow morning.' In the next breath, he reminded me of the list of things to bring along from home for his soccer practice. Immediately after I had finished the conversation with him and had put down my phone, it rang for the second time. It was Aaron again, asking me what time I would be picking him up the next morning. 'And don't forget to bring my socks,' he added.

It was obvious that he was anxious, as he was not at home to be in control of the situation and to make sure that all the paraphernalia that he needed for his soccer game the next day would be there. He usually made sure the night before that everything was in order for the next day. He was clearly worried that I might forget some of the items.

Early the next morning, at about seven o'clock, he called again, just in case I had forgotten about the time. 'Aaron,'

I asked him, 'why are you up so early? Did you sleep at all the whole night?' He replied that he had gotten up early and was unable to get back to sleep.

Though anxious, he had already overcome his rigidity to keep to a fixed routine. His staying over at the grandparents' house was unplanned, and nobody had told him beforehand about the change of plans.

Turning the clock back six years into the past, the same scenario would have created a massive tantrum for Aaron. Though the residual symptoms of his over-anxiousness are seen every now and then, they are within normal limits and are much more controlled. His adaptability to a sudden change of routine and his easy-going flexibility today is nothing short of a miracle to me.

4. Too detailed recall

Aaron's sister was reading *Harry Potter and the Goblet of Fire* and was lamenting that it was such a thick book with so many pages. Immediately, Aaron corrected her and said, 'It's not the thickest book, you know, Alysha. It has only 636 pages. Do you know that *Harry Potter and the Order of the Phoenix* has about 766 pages?' Out of curiosity, I asked him if he remembered the number of pages of all the other Harry Potter books that he had read. Amazingly, he did, and he rattled off the titles of the other books in the order of their length. 'The third longest books are *Harry Potter and the Deathly Hallows* and *Harry Potter and the Half-Blood Prince* – both 606 pages. The rest of the books are shorter. *Harry Potter and the Prisoner of Azkaban* has 317 pages. *Harry Potter and the Chamber of Secrets* and *Harry Potter*

A Rude Awakening for a Boy with Autism

and the Philosopher's Stone are shorter – between 200 to 300 pages. I'm not sure about the last two books.' I asked him if he also knew the chronological order of the books. It was obvious that he did; the sequence was clearly imprinted in his mind, and he gave me the list correctly.

Aaron's remarkable memory for details was not only reflected in his accurate recollection of the number of pages and the chronological sequence of the books in the *Harry Potter* series but also in his vivid recall of the pages where specific incidents of the plot took place. However, his skewed memory for details posed a challenge to him when he could not sift the important details from the story. To condense the story to a few sentences was a challenge to him. It blew his mind to determine which details were too insignificant to be included in the main plot. He was always tongue-tied when asked to tell briefly the gist of the story he had read. He had absolutely no idea where to begin and where to end unless someone asked him some leading questions.

5. Too rigid adherence to rules

After taking his lunch one day, his good friend invited him to play for a short while. He agreed, and the two boys left their lunch boxes on the ledge near the canteen while they disappeared to play. When they returned just before the bell rang, the discipline master was there waiting for them. They were reprimanded for having left their things around. As a punishment, they had to go around the school compound to pick up rubbish. As a result, they missed the Christian fellowship that they were looking forward to attending. The double trouble drove Aaron to tears. To Aaron, being law biding, breaking a rule in itself was a heartbreaking offense to him, and to be reprimanded for it was like adding fuel to the fire.

Aaron's strengths

Aaron's memory for details, coupled with his intense power of concentration, helped him not just in detailed mind mapping of road directions but also in chess tournaments. The following incident below illustrates this.

After defeating his opponent in the earlier knockout rounds, a boy was heard remarking about Aaron to another would-be contestant, 'Watch out for him. He is really good.'

At the semi-finals, Aaron competed against the former runner-up in his school. Aaron was calm and composed throughout the duration of the game, unruffled by the distracting grunts and remarks of his opponent. Nor did the emotion-charged atmosphere around him affect him. He was truly focused. He took his time, thinking carefully of his strategies and moves. His cool collected attitude seemed to be his added advantage. He defeated his opponent to get into the finals.

At the finals, however, the incumbent reigning champion for several years was too good and experienced of an opponent for him. Aaron lost in the finals. Considering that he was still a novice in the game, with just one year's experience, he couldn't have asked for more than being the runner-up!

In school, his class teacher reported that Aaron was a popular and gentle boy. He was said to be painstaking and industrious in his work. The teachers had no problems with him in his conduct. His best subject was mathematics, and he was and still is in the Australian Mathematical Olympiad.

A tribute to Aaron

At my friend's fortieth birthday celebration recently, she gave a heart-warming speech in which she mentioned that she had always looked upon Aaron as her highest inspiration for her son, who is also autistic. She was in the throes of raising her three-and-a-half-year-old autistic son, similar to the position I was in several years ago. She offered the highest tribute to Aaron. It made me think that God has given me Aaron for such a purpose as this.

Overall, I can only say that Aaron's brain is wired differently from ours. What is natural and intuitive for us can be overwhelming for him, and vice versa. I believe he will continue to learn, adapt, and function in this real world, which is rather confusing and irrational to him. In fact, he has largely acquired the 'language' of this world, even though it is not his 'native language'. In other words, he is in the process of unlocking a maze that leads to his highest goal – to be perceived as a non-autistic person in the eyes of the world.

PART THREE
AT PRESENT

CHAPTER 12:
Aaron As He Is Today, Aged Fifteen

CHAPTER 12

AARON AS HE IS TODAY (AGED FIFTEEN)

'Aaron is so normal. Looks like he is autistic no more.' I smiled, though the words 'He really is not what you see on the outside' almost slipped out of my lips. My tacit response spared me of a lengthy explanation, especially for one who had no clue about autism. Besides, the subject did not befit the social occasion.

It has been four years since the last chapter of this book was written, when Aaron was eleven. An interested reader may be curious to know what further changes have taken place since then. In this last write-up, I will get past the easy, convenient glib response to a place of complete honesty. I will describe Aaron as he is, with his milestones of progress, as well as the challenges and hurdles that still constantly plague him.

At fifteen, Aaron is a warm, easy-going, and amiable youth, exuding a spirit of gentleness and quiet confidence. He is not easily ruffled or agitated, being more in control of his emotions. The episodes linked to his inflexibility, anxiety disorder and antisocial behaviour, are a thing of the past. Though not particularly articulate, he certainly is not reticent and withdrawn like before. He makes a conscious effort to interact and communicate, having acquired the skills of exchanging pleasantries and social etiquette. Friendly and well mannered, he expresses himself so well that it belies his innate inadequacy. It is not his second nature, however, to enjoy a prolonged tête-à-tête, especially when it is haphazard, unstructured, and touches on anything under the sun. A juxtaposition of unrelated pieces of information and questions thrown together in a casual conversation unsettles him. It demands tremendous effort on his part to concentrate on and manage a long conversation, as his thoughts naturally wander away. His mind seems to shut down naturally when he reaches the point of information overload, so he drifts into the comfort zone of his daydreams.

The intrinsic problem is that his mind perceives every minute detail as important. To see the wood for the trees and to sieve the necessary parts from the irrelevant, disconnected, and unstructured details have always posed a great challenge to him.

Aaron's keen eye for specific details (even those minutiae that we often skim or gloss over as unimportant or irrelevant) causes him to frequently miss out on the central principles, their applications, and the relationships between them. Without the wisdom to discriminate unnecessary details, he is slow in completing the experiments for his science practical in school. It does not help that he also takes more time than normal in processing and comprehending the many instructions given to him at one time.

Interestingly, his meticulousness over details is not transferred or reflected in his writing or his schoolwork. He doesn't write the alphabet clearly; his writing is generally untidy and illegible. He doesn't do his workbook painstakingly, with neat straight lines on the left side of the page. A fussy teacher who was particular about neatness and sidelines once marked him down for his overall effort.

In his creative composition in English, his teacher considered his ideas too 'outside the box' at times. He once described the adventures of a boy who had a peculiar obsession (chasing and catching butterflies) which resulted in the dire consequence of his getting lost in the forest. Though it was well-written prose, he lost marks on the rather unusual and unconventional subject matter.

Aaron is still very literal in his understanding of words or statements. Though he has learnt some idioms and figurative expressions, he still struggles with the skill of inferring. A simple question like 'What is the colour of your car?' may baffle him, as his too literal mind tells him that the question is irrelevant because he does not own a car. He does not naturally deduce that the question is referring to his parents' car, the car he has been travelling in, since he is not expected to own one, being too young to drive or to have a licence.

He also stumbles over questions that are open-ended, too general and abstract. His mind thinks in terms of specifics, broken-down segments of the whole, as well as in concrete visual images. Faced with questions that defy his natural patterns of thinking, he is befuddled and stuck. In examinations, he attempts to make an intelligent guess which can sometimes miss the mark.

Aaron relates to a large circle of acquaintances and casual friends from his school and the church, despite not being communication savvy. Among the few buddies he is closer to, his best friend is one who shares common interests, likes and dislikes, and speaks a similar 'language' as him. As they mutually understand each other, Aaron is most himself and at ease with him. Being more articulate than Aaron, he possibly has Asperger's syndrome.

In his class this year, there are many new students, both boys and girls. On the first day of school, he unabashedly singled out those who were bashful or felt left out and extended his hand of friendship and hospitality to them. As an old student of the school, he took upon himself the responsibility of welcoming the new ones into the school, quite unlike his old self. He even went the second mile and accompanied a new student to a uniform shop outside the main complex of the school to get some stationery. It was during the short lunch break. As a result, he missed his lunch!

Overall, he does well in school. He is among the top in mathematics, his best and favourite subject. He also excels in chess, and he has won several awards in tournaments. His forte is also in computer skills. Knowing the way he thinks, based on logic and governed by set parameters, it's hardly surprising that he exhibits unusual competence in these subjects. In stark contrast is his lack in coordination and gross motor skills; hence his weakest subject is sports and physical education.

Aaron is quite an angel at home. Unlike many teenagers, he does not gripe, complain, or behave rebelliously when given instructions to follow. He is compliant and cooperative most of the time. On the flip side, he lacks the initiative to fill his free time well and constructively. Unless he is given clear instructions, he is quite glad to be lost in his own world of imagination or to indulge in his favourite hobby – surfing the net for free software to be downloaded into his computer. He is gadget and technologically hip, like most others of his digital generation.

Aaron has not been open to disclosing his autism spectrum to his teachers in school. Many of them are still unaware of it, except for a few whom I used my discretion to inform, like his physical education teacher. This year, however, in the upper secondary, every student has been assigned a special teacher cum tutor who is the bridge between the parent and the school. Each tutor meets twice a week with about fifteen students under his or her pastoral care.

Aaron and I met up with his pastoral teacher at the end of last year. I suggested to Aaron that he should confide in his teacher about his autism, which he subsequently did, albeit quite reluctantly. If all spectrums of his autism had dissipated through the years without any residual effect, my suggestion would be deemed most unwise and insensitive. He has always felt safer and less vulnerable keeping his autism private, as the stigma of being different always bothers him. When his teacher asked if he had anything special to share with her in confidence, he struggled and hesitated before he finally plucked up his courage to say, rather incoherently, 'I have autism.' For Aaron to mention the formidable truth openly for the first time was unnerving; it was like letting out a well-guarded and sacred secret which he had tried and worked so hard to conceal from public view and knowledge. His teacher was pleased that he informed her about his condition, for it would certainly help her give him the appropriate guidance and assistance should he need it.

I must also mention Aaron's love for God. He is consistent and disciplined in his devotions and prayers. In his Christian Studies recently, he was asked to write about his testimony and biography. While pondering on how to make his story interesting, it dawned on him to write about his autism. He mentioned that it was in the year 2010 that God became very real to him. He used to think like a perfectionist and could not believe or accept his own failings and mistakes. It gradually dawned on him that his innate perception of people and the world at large was out of line. He confessed that he thought he was the one normal among quirky and abnormal people. In 2010, he experienced a 'rude awakening', a paradigm shift, in his vision of the real world. It became clearer, as if seen from borrowed lenses. He has since learned how not to be a square peg in a round hole. He has overcome most of his inborn eccentricities so well that he is proud and happy to say that he is now normal. To me, it is heart-warming to know that he has learned to embrace his past and his autism.

He had always wanted to be baptized, and my husband and I decided to make it a special one for him and his sister, Alysha, in the Jordan River in Israel. We made our trip there as a church group during the long holidays in December 2013, in the midst of a cold winter.

Aaron was eagerly looking forward to his baptism, undeterred by the foreboding weather and the icy waters of the Jordan River. When the day arrived, he was to be the fifth and last candidate to be baptised. The baptism ceremony was short and crisp, as no one would want to stay any longer in the water than necessary. But not Aaron! When his turn came, he was in no hurry to make his confession of faith to be followed by a quick dip. He made sure that his baptism was complete with his litany of praise to God and thanksgiving to his parents, the church, and others who had helped him in his faith. He was not deterred by the cold, nor was he embarrassed, to make his speech openly and publicly. It didn't matter that he was the only one of the candidates to do something different. He'd made up his mind that his baptism was not complete without going through the whole procedure, and nothing could stop him from going through with it.

The pastors could not help but praise him for his fervent and sincere attempt. Possibly quivering under their skins in the cold, they intermittently commended Aaron by saying, 'Very good, very good', perhaps secretly hoping that Aaron would shorten his speech. If so, their hints to Aaron fell flat. Aaron was even more inspired to continue his speech without any reservation. When it was finally over, he was greeted with a loud reverberating applause. It was such a memorable and spiritually uplifting experience for Aaron. As for the pastors, they must have felt a great sense of relief and accomplishment too – especially for having lasted so long in the cold.

Even though he has overcome most of his obsessions and routine-bound rigidities, Aaron still battles some challenges of autism that contravene the norm. It is as if he is trying hard and is determined to reprogram the way he is naturally wired in order to operate in a dimension like everyone else.

I recall the days of his childhood when the slightest incident that caused him to feel different or excluded could drive him to tears, even when the waiter of a restaurant removed all the menus from the table except the kids' menu that was with him. He has come a long way since then. It is a continuous process of acquiring and learning more cognitive and living skills to blend in with the social environment that is natural for others but rather counter-intuitive for him. His human spirit has triumphed against all odds, to fight his way out of the cage of his disorder and to be liberated from the stereotyped label. In short, he has publicly and officially lost his autism stigma. He is coping well, and I have the confidence that 'all I have seen teaches me to trust the Creator for all I have not seen' (Ralph Waldo Emerson).

Looking back, my journey with Aaron was not devoid of tumultuous times, fraught with moments of anger, anxiety, disappointment, and self-doubt. Of all that God has taught me through it, the most precious lesson I can learn from it is that none of our pain and suffering is wasted if we choose to let God use such things for His redemptive purpose. I believe that whatever the outcome of our struggles may be, there is always fruit in adversity, the intensity of which is in direct proportion – the greater the adversity, the sweeter the fruit. As for me, I can see the unravelling of God's plan in His promise that He 'comforts us in all our troubles so that we can comfort those in any trouble with the comfort we ourselves have received from God' (2 Cor. 1:3– 4). He has birthed in me a new gifting and ministry that was never mine before – to be the bridge of God's grace, hope, comfort, and physical help to others going through similar struggles like mine. What I baulked at years ago have turned out to be rich experiences and resources that have equipped me for this ministry.

I must admit, however, that oftentimes I do not have the answers, especially for those whose hopes and expectations for their children have been dashed when they see not progress but only more temper tantrums and aggressive behaviour as the child approaches adolescence. Putting myself in their shoes, would I not have been just as angry and frustrated? Possibly so, for I am only human. I wouldn't dare to be outrageously presumptuous that I would be any different. But given the situation, what choice have I but to cling desperately to God for His sustaining grace and patience, even when there are no visible results? Should I falter, I would want to pick up the pieces again. Through the gruelling process of pressing on against all odds, I hope to become that bright and shining gem glowing in the dark and tested by the fire. If nothing ever changes at the end of it all, at least the adversity is the making of me (with much value-added impact), peeling off the layers of self and pride and bringing out the best in me!

As a postscript, I would like to include a write-up by Aaron himself, at the age of fifteen-plus. It reflects his thoughts, feelings, and journey of faith.

At 8.30 p.m. on 28 June 1998, I came bursting in the world, kicking and screaming. My parents described me then as having a very strong pair of lungs. I was ready to take on the world!

At the age of three and still unable to speak, doctors diagnosed me with autism. My parents were told that autism was a lifelong disability. I went to autistic schools in my early years, and through intensive therapy, I learnt to talk and engage in simple activities others took for granted, like playing on a see-saw and swing.

I had autistic abilities of uncanny road map reading skills and instantly identifying the day of the week in any year named. However, I found it hard to cope with changes. Social situations terrified me and caused me to scream incessantly. I also had an obsession with road signs and would stare at them from all angles for hours on end.

My family did not cease praying for me, and by the grace of God, I responded to the intensive therapy in school. I started speaking and gradually learnt to cope with many things I found difficult before. The autistic traits became less noticeable through the primary school years. The autism in me was something only God could help me lose, so it has strengthened my family's Christian faith. Today, having autism in my early life is my largest secret.

I have settled well in my current school and am enjoying school because of the great facilities available. I play basketball and soccer as my school sports, but sports not being my forte meant I have always been on the lowest team. I also play chess for my school and have entered many tournaments, the most memorable being the Australian Junior Championships this year.

To sum up my personal beliefs, I am a Christian. I regularly attend the Friday evening church youth group and Sunday morning worship services. Being born into a Christian family has helped me know of God's love for me since I was young. However, the reality of His love and how He has always been with me and helped me in my journey with autism was the deciding factor in giving my life to God in 2010. I was baptised last year during the summer holidays in the Jordan River, where Jesus himself was baptised. This was one of the most special moments I have ever had. My spiritual understanding has been significantly shaped by a church tour to Israel, where I visited the places where biblical events occurred and I realised how authentic the Bible is.

As I finish writing the past events of my life, I ruminate about what the school chaplain said on orientation day, which definitely reflects my current outlook on life: 'There's more to me than that.' Looking back, I can hardly believe what I used to be like.

A Sibling's Perspective of Aaron

(Alysha's recall of her feelings and thoughts, growing up as Aaron's younger sister)

I am about two years younger than Aaron, but many think that I am older because of how I behave. I grew up defending and caring for him, especially when other children did not understand him and his actions. Having stronger hands, I helped him with practical things such as opening the lids of containers.

Aaron used to have therapies at home and outside. I had always thought that having therapy sessions was necessary for every child. When Aaron was seated with his therapist at home, he insisted that I sit together with him throughout the session. I did not make too much fuss about it because I thought it was part of my routine. However, at the therapy sessions, I was not allowed to answer any questions asked – I was just to accompany him and be silent. Sometimes I could not help napping on the table while the therapy was going on.

We each had a Megasketcher (drawing board) which we used to write and draw on.

Aaron and Alysha and their Megasketchers

I remember an incident when I was just over three years old. Aaron liked to watch *Toy Story*, and his favourite line that he repeatedly wrote and shouted was 'To infinity and beyond!' I followed his example but could not pronounce 'infinity' accurately or spell it correctly. I used to spell it as 'infiniti'. He was very mad with me, and each time I made the mistake, he shouted at me and even kicked me. I just could not get it right, especially with my pronunciation. He had no mercy or patience with me, even though I was just a little girl. Because he was hard on me, I learnt to be accurate in my spelling as I grew up. Today we are both quite competent in spelling.

Although we were very close, we had a little sibling rivalry. I wondered why I had to be the one to give in to Aaron most of the time – I thought it was not fair. When I woke up earlier than Aaron in the morning, I was not allowed to leave the bed until Aaron was up, and he had to be the first to leave the bedroom. When we were playing games like Snakes and Ladders, he did not want to lose. He always had to be the winner, but gradually he learnt to be a good loser when he learnt to convince himself that 'it was not a race'.

We enjoyed playing a lot of made-up games together, but most of them were quite repetitive. We created our own stories and imaginary characters. We made a lot of noise, and I always had fun playing these games. I found myself imitating Aaron in many ways, such as copying him by drawing in the air with my finger. Mum had to teach me that I didn't need to be like Aaron, so I didn't need to do whatever he did. I also picked up from Aaron the ability to write words and sentences reflecting the mirror image. We did it occasionally just for fun. Only the two of us could understand easily what we wrote, but most adults would need a mirror to decipher it.

By the time I was in preschool, I'd developed a stubborn nature. I refused to put on many dresses that my mum wanted me to wear. I had my own mind. During the parents' day at preschool, I refused to take part in the concert. My parents and grandparents were disappointed when they saw that I was the only one not dressed colourfully and that I was seated on the stage while everyone else was dancing energetically. All my other friends entertained the audience while I was just looking around. I wonder if, as my mum had said, that my obstinate behaviour could be a reaction to Aaron getting more attention than me.

I was about six years old when Aaron's speech pathologist said to me, 'Say sausage.' I felt left out having no therapy, so I pronounced it as 'thauthage', with a purposely accentuated lisp. I was put into speech therapy for several months, but while having the sessions, I came to the realisation that I shouldn't continue trying to be like Aaron.

When I was younger, I did not like Aaron to get more attention than I did because it made me feel neglected and unhappy. Today, as a teenager, I understand why Aaron needed more attention. We have become great buddies, and he helps me a lot with my homework. He has a very good sense of direction, unlike me, so he always knows where to go.

Overall, Aaron has been a great brother to me, and we have become very close. Without many words being said, we always find ourselves understanding each other. Looking back, I didn't get to enjoy the typical playing that other children might have experienced, having a loving sibling relationship that other children might have enjoyed, or learning another language. But I don't even recall ever thinking that Aaron was different from any other child. My relationship with Aaron has come to be much stronger than many other sibling relationships because of the countless hours we spent playing together, us always looking out for each other and even going to therapy together. I wouldn't exchange that for the whole world.

Alysha – 'I wouldn't exchange that for the whole world.'

Aaron's Present Explanation of Some of His Past Eccentric Behaviour and Hypersensitivities

These additional notes are added to help parents of children with autism (especially those who have limited verbal communication) know that there is always a reason why the child is screaming or is upset, even if they cannot see any rhyme or reason for that to occur. Assuming that the child may be similar to Aaron in some ways, the additional facts may give parents a clue to the problems or puzzles they face. Aaron, almost sixteen years old at the time of publication and being articulate, is able to explain why those situations upset him when he was younger. Had I known the reasons then, I would have been much better able to cope.

1. Haircuts and nail cutting

Aaron used to scream uncontrollably whenever his hair was cut. Not only were the strands of hair falling on his neck and shoulder itchy and irritating, but he could also feel the pain each time I held his hair to be cut. To him, the slightest tug or sensation on his head felt like a knife cutting him. His head was probably hypersensitive, which also explains why he did not like his head getting wet. Similarly, he resisted having his nails cut for the same reason; it was unbearable pain to his hypersensitive skin.

2. Tears and getting wet

He did not like the sensation of wetness on his face, and he was too young to understand that the more upset he was, the more his tears flowed. At a later age, he also saw on the TV how tears would ruin the look of someone's face, hence his hatred for it.

Aaron did not like the sensation of being wet, especially his feet. His feet are particularly sensitive and feel extremely uncomfortable when they are wet. His abnormally heightened sensation in his feet makes them many times more sensitive than most of us. Even now, his feet are still very sensitive, so much so that any touch will make him cringe and feel highly ticklish.

3. Aversions to certain food

He could not make himself eat 'runny' half-boiled eggs and Nutella because he saw the egg and chocolate stains smeared all over his sister's mouth when she took them. Being extremely visual, he could not stand the ghastly sight which looked like a disfigured face to him. He could not imagine taking it himself and looking anything like that. His sister also took some fish balls and comically puffed up her cheeks with them, thereby distorting her mouth. It was also a disgusting sight to him. Since then, he cannot bring himself to eat any fish balls.

4. Pets

Aaron used to be terrified of dogs. He was so terrified that he dared not enter a friend's house where there were dogs roaming in the compound. He had to be carried all the way into the house. He said it was because he read a book about a ferocious dog with fangs. The vivid visual image in his mind instilled the phobia in him. His phobia for dogs was also extended to other pets with fangs, like cats. He overcame it recently when he got used to our family's pet dog, Coco, a poodle. It was therapeutic to him.

5. Finger writing in the air

When Aaron was still in the primary school, he had the habit of finger writing and drawing in the air. He explained that he could only think visually and doing that helped him in his thinking process.

6. Labels

a) House numbers and signs

Aaron said that he had a fixation that everything needed a label. For commercial buildings, the labels were either the board sign or the shop number. As for residential houses, the label was the house number. Any house without a number meant that it was not labelled. In his mind, it did not conform to the norm or general rule and was therefore not acceptable. It was 'senseless' to him, and therefore he should not enter it.

This explains why he was so adamant about looking at the house number in Carlingford before he could enter the house (refer to chapter 7(b)). It was not right for him to enter through the garage because there was no house number there. It is a new discovery even for me, right now. All the while, I thought he was only routine bound and wanted to follow a fixed route into the house. I know now that the more important reason to him was that he had to make sure the label or the number of the house was there before it made sense for him to enter it.

(b) Exit signs
The exit sign was also a label that he needed to make sense of the countless entrances in the shopping malls. Every exit was marked and therefore he would not enter a store without an exit sign. He felt assured and secure to enter only if he could spot the sign(s).

[Out of all the signs, I asked him why the GIVE WAY sign was his favourite. He explained that it was the most visually appealing of all the signs and therefore he liked it.]

Labels were Aaron's way of making sense of the real world; that was probably why he responded well with the PECS (picture exchange communication system), a system of communication which Giant Steps enforced as part of his therapy and communication. He brought his PECS everywhere in a little booklet, which was strung over his neck with a string so that he could pull the picture out of the Velcro each time he needed to let anyone know what he wanted. That was the right 'click', or signal, for him to start communicating with the world. Consequently, he gradually emerged out of his own world. This might not work for other autistic children, but as for Aaron, we were fortunate to have discovered the key which Aaron needed to unlock himself out of his world of non-verbal communication.

APPENDIX

FREQUENTLY ASKED QUESTIONS (FAQS)

B elow are some of the questions that were frequently posed to me. I'm basing answers on my experience and basic knowledge of the subject. For more detailed medical explanation, please refer to the experts.

1. How could the paediatrician tell that Aaron was autistic? Can you share what you have seen and learnt about the common indicators and characteristics of autism?

Answer: The paediatrician specialising in autism observed and tested Aaron based on a list of criteria for identifying the various spectrums of autism. In Aaron's case, the diagnosis was made in one session, after she had observed him for a few hours. She could identify about ten classic symptoms or manifestations of the syndrome quite quickly. For other children who do not manifest such obvious symptoms, the process may take a few sessions before any conclusion can be made.

These are some examples I know about some common indicators. The child does not

a. use his or her index finger to point to ask or to indicate interest in something,
b. take an interest in other children,
c. enjoy the 'pretend' game,
d. make eye contact with you,
e. enjoy being hugged or bounced on your knees, and
f. usually look across to see an interesting object you are pointing at, even after you have his or her attention.

According to some autism specialists, sensory problems are also common with autism. Issues may vary, as can the degree of severity, but the majority of children with autism have at least one sensory disorder, be it tactile, auditory, visual, taste, olfactory, vestibular (movement and gravity), or proprioceptive sensitivities (joint muscle and body awareness).

The autism experts also identify the common characteristics as follows:

a. Delays and deficits in acquiring speech and language
b. Poor interaction with others and lack of understanding of social interactions
c. Unusual responses to the environment (e.g., hypersensitivity to noise)
d. A need for precise routines and sameness in the environment

e. Self-stimulatory behaviour (e.g., hand flapping and tapping – referred to as 'stimming')
f. Impaired intellectual functioning, often with isolated special skills

2. From a man's point of view, how did Aaron's father respond to his son being diagnosed as autistic?

Answer (by Aaron's father): Being in the medical field, I could tell from the early stage of Aaron's development as a child that he was different. I noticed some abnormality in his behaviour, such as having no eye contact and being emotionally detached and non-verbal. However, I hoped that the symptoms would just go away.

When he was finally diagnosed as displaying autistic symptoms, I wasn't too surprised. Yet I wasn't prepared to accept the unwelcome news. I hoped that the diagnosis was wrong and the symptoms would eventually go away.

Like people going through grief, I too went through the typical four stages of (a) denial, (b) anger, (c) guilt and pain, and (d) acceptance. In the initial state of denial, I kept telling myself that Aaron was normal like anyone else, and I was consciously, though unconvincingly, deluding myself that the diagnosis was a big mistake. Then, when the reality sank in, I was angry. I had to live with the stigma that my child was not normal and the dreams and plans I had for my child were unlikely to be fulfilled. I was also gripped with the agonising thought of having to face endless needs and pressures in the future. There were days I was plagued by thoughts of guilt, wondering whether I had actually done wrong to deserve such a 'punishment'. When I came to the last stage of acceptance, I became extremely desperate to look for a quick fix to the problem. I wasted no time in exploring the possible alternatives on the Internet, looking for some effective therapies or early intervention programs to do the job. I had to settle with the fact that the process would be a long and painstaking one and there were no guarantees either. Every child is an individual, and I do recognise that what works for one child may not work for another.

I decided to eliminate some of the options available, based on reason and the cost of the therapy. Though I had accepted Aaron's condition, I still struggled with occasional lapses of anger and pain, especially in the initial years, when Aaron's progress did not hit the development benchmarks. I can say that for a number of years, I had not fully come to terms with Aaron's autism.

It was only when Aaron was showing many positive signs of being able to function normally, when he was about six years of age, that I can really say that I had fully accepted Aaron's syndrome and even felt completely positive about it.

3. *Was Aaron on any special diet as is often recommended for autistic children?*

Answer: Aaron was on a gluten- and dairy-free diet for a short period, about a month. As there didn't seem to be any noticeable change in his behaviour, we decided to take him off the diet. We concluded that he didn't have a leaky gut syndrome, as is quite common with autistic children, and so it was unnecessary for him to continue with the diet. As he was already so picky about his food, taking him off the diet did relieve us of the additional stress we had to put up with in just getting him to eat. However, he was on soya milk instead of cow's milk for a few years. As he grew up, he was adaptable to both. He enjoys food, and he is eating freely. We did give him supplementary vitamins specially developed for autistic children in the early years.

4. *What therapies did Aaron go through?*

Answer: In his special school, Aaron went through an individualised program using a trans-disciplinary approach. In this program, various therapies specific to each child's needs and activities are taught collaboratively. They are as follows:

- Music therapy
- Speech pathology
- Living skills
- Occupational therapy
- Play therapy
- Special education or academics

Through the music therapy, the child integrates his auditory, cognitive, motor, and social skills. Through the speech pathology, the child learns social communicative skills and interaction skills. Through the living skills, the child learns the basic skills like dressing, road safety and making purchases. Through the occupational therapy, the child improves on his bilateral motor coordination, eye-hand coordination, and motor planning essential for the development of gross motor play. Finally, through the academics, the child improves on his cognitive development, fine motor skills, and play skills.

Besides these therapies offered in his special school, Aaron had additional therapies to improve his skills in speech, play, and academics. At the latest stage, when he was between six to eight years of age, he went through the RDI (Relational Development Intervention) therapy. I believe Aaron improved in his skills in emotional referencing and relational information processing through RDI.

He learned to obtain meaning based upon the larger context through the use of inferring skills in language as well as in non-verbal communication. It helped him to engage in meaningful communication in his interaction with his peers and others.

5. *What comments, from your experience, are helpful for one to say to mothers of autistic children and what are not?*

Answer: Many of my Christian friends often used some common Christian clichés to comfort me in my struggles, but to be frank, they did not help. In fact, they made me feel worse. They gave words of advice like 'God knows', 'If you have enough faith and trust in God, He will work things out for you', and 'God has chosen you to have a special child because He knows you can handle it'. Their comments, however well intended, sounded hollow to me and lacked the tenderness that could only resonate through personal experience and knowledge.

A friend tried to comfort me by saying that she had gone through similar struggles and that God was faithful to see her through. She sounded hollow to me, as I thought that her child had only a minor physical defect. How could her struggle in seeing to her child be compared to my struggle of raising an autistic child? Her good intentions to console me backfired then, for all I perceived was that she was downplaying the seriousness of my situation and was almost implying that I shouldn't feel so stressed because I had God to help me. I felt it was an irrelevant comparison. To be fair to her, however, she was sincere when she compared her struggles with mine. In her eyes, the defect of her child was a major lifelong problem and her intention was truly to encourage me and not to trivialize my struggle.

I would have preferred my friends to say nothing but just be there for me. In my opinion, this is the best thing to say: 'Is there any practical way I can help?' Then they could do whatever they could within their constraints of time, finances, and so forth.

6. *How do you think your journey has helped you in your personal growth? Has it helped you to enrich the lives of those who are presently going through similar struggles?*

Answer: Because I had been through the same struggle, I am not insulated from their pain and can offer not just sympathy but empathetic attachment. I have developed the patience to listen to all their woes, frustration, and complaints with my heart and not just with my ears, and I am able to offer whatever practical counsel which, through my experience, had been helpful. I am presently helping a friend by cooking a meal for her family at least once a week and babysitting her autistic child whenever I can so that she can have a break to do her shopping or just to have a relief from her stress.

7. Did your child go through the ABA (applied behaviour analysis) method of intensive behavioural intervention? Do you think it is effective?

My son didn't, but I know of some who have gone through it and found it effective. From the report made by the Autism Society of America, the ABA method consists of a lot of structure and reinforcement, using precise teaching techniques. The goal is to minimise the child's failures and maximise his successes in learning and acquiring new behaviours and skills. The program is highly structured and tailored for the individual needs of the child.